Live Worthy

Choosing to Live Worthy of His Name.

Daily Devotions for Those Desiring to Live Radically

1st Timothy

Tammy Conner Stearns

Live Worthy

Live Worthy: Choosing to Live Worthy of His Name

Authored by Tammy Conner Stearns

6" x 9" (15.24 x 22.86 cm)

Black & White on White paper

257 pages

ISBN-10: 1794117830

Copyright © 2019 by Tammy Jo Stearns

All rights reserved. This book or any portion thereof may not be reproduced or used in any manner whatsoever without the express written permission of the publisher except for the use of brief quotations in a book review.

Printed in the United States of America

Unless otherwise noted, Scripture taken from the HOLY BIBLE, NEW INTERNATIONAL VERSION. Copyright 1973, 1978, 1984 by International Bible Society. Used by permission of Zondervan. All rights reserved.

First Printing, 2019

Tammy Stearns

Project H.O.P.E.

1419 S Enterprise

Springfield, MO 65804

stearnstammy@ymail.com

Ordering Information:

Quantity sales. Special discounts are available on quantity purchases by corporations, associations, and others. For details, contact the author at the address above.

Regarding 'Know Hope'

"It has been my privilege to know and work alongside the Stearns family in Nicaragua on many short term mission trips over the past 10 years. You get to know a person real well when you get dirty and sweaty on a daily basis all the while sharing the same goal: care for others with great joy! I can personally vouch for this amazing, inspiring family and their selfless life decision to serve the least of these. Through what most of us would consider insurmountable, heartbreaking circumstances, Tammy Conner Stearns and her husband have continued to know hope. Hope that maintains and encourages a weary traveler through daily life. Supernatural Hope. Hope from the Heavenly Father to his children. Hope eternal."

Mary Ann....

"A must read devotional no matter where you are in your journey of faith. If you are going through a difficult time or have gone through the valley in the past and you need encouragement you will want to read this. Thank you Stearns family for living out your faith in a real, authentic way in the midst of a tragedy that reveals a Father who is real and faithful. Thank you for writing down your journey to help others!"

Anonymous....

"I loved everything about this book. Tammy's (author) ability to seek and speak truth from this tragedy is nothing less than inspiring. It has become my favorite daily devotional."

Shelley G.....

"Beautiful!"

Pam Jolliff..

"I intended to use this book as a devotional. Once I started reading, I just couldn't stop. I was reading on the plane and people probably thought I was nuts with tears flowing down my face. What a testimony and encouragement Tammy is. Now that I am done, I will go back and use as a devotional, meditating on the verses and the wise words in this book. I am inspired and challenged all at the same time. Thank you Tammy and Travis for living worthy and shining the light of Christ. He is definitely glorified!"

Kristy Stillwell....

"Tammy's writing is simply amazing. She shares from her heart in such an authentic and encouraging way. Without sugar coating things, it's clear that she has an everlasting hope that lies in far more than anything this world can offer. Through her life, struggles and faithfulness I've learned so much and cherish all of those lessons. I can't stop thinking of friends I want to share this book with...I've bought 3 copies so far, and already need more!"

Hannah Wingo....

"Incredible how God is using Tae's life.... with your gifted writing, providing His insights and profound truths..... You are an inspiration to all."

Jo Burden....

"Knowing Tammy personally, the books reads as if she is talking directly to me! Love it!"

Ted....

"Tammy Conner Stearns, you taught me as a mother how to walk through grief in such a way that glorified God. To read your most personal thoughts as you walked the road of Taellor's death brought me such comfort. Your words gave me encouragement for whatever I may face in the days to come. Thank you for being obedient to our God and giving Hope to all those around you."

Laurie Sutton Moudy....

"You gave me strength while I was going through a rough time in my life. Your words and scriptures you posted lifted me up and gave me courage to face another day!! I do appreciate your willingness to share your thoughts, prayers, hope and faith. You have no idea how many people your positive words and example encouraged and renewed. Thank you."

Vicki Luttrull Rhodes....

"I will never forget landing in Nicaragua and being greeted by Taellor. I was loaded with a heavy backpack full of things for serving. Taellor immediately took my backpack off my back and placed it on hers. She had a BIG smile on her face as I explained it was too heavy for her. Needless to say, I made a connection with her immediately. As I watched her work, I have never seen a young person so gifted or humble in working with the people, especially the children. She was mature beyond her years. The love of Christ poured out of her, touching everyone she came in contact with. I know Taellor was what she was because of her mother, Tammy, and God. Tammy is so rich in every way, and I am so looking forward to her book. Her writings have taught me much."

                                                        Tibby Martin....

"INSPIRATIONAL!"

                                                        Mike G....

"There are few people who can write the Truth and sound as if they are merely a friend guiding you down a path. Tammy does this. She opens up her life and lets us have a peek inside while sharing the depth of the valley of grief that none of us wish to ever walk. The death of a child is hard enough but to decide to grieve in a Godly-way while still in this world is most difficult. I have devoured Know Hope and cannot wait for the next one!"

                                                Maria N.........

"My mom is like someone who can usually explain things really well. "

                                          Slaton S..... (11 yrs old)

Live Worthy

A Daily Devotion for Those Who are Seeking to Live Worthy

Thank you, to so many, who came beside us in obedience when we found ourselves deep in the valley and continue to walk this journey of faithful obedience with us. For those who are the family of our faith that He has given us, without you, life here would look so incredibly different. I dare say that each person that opens this cover deserves their name on this page for you have been a part of our journey.

Thank you to our Project H.O.P.E. family and Ridgecrest Baptist Church for being willing to "step outside the box" and encourage and equip leading us all on a journey that only God could write.

Thank you to our staff at HOPE Central, Center of Hope, UnShackled and Taellor's House that we serve with daily.

Thank you for those who continued to encourage me to write and publish this. As I have always said, these aren't my words but His. But, thank you, for without each of you prodding me along, this probably would not have ever came to fruition. Hazel, your messages and phone calls of encouragement were treasured more than you will ever know.

Thank you to Sarah and Stephanie, for being that circle.

Thank you to Annie, "that girl", who will forever be imprinted on our lives. The very best friend that Tae could have had.

Thank you to Claudia, Meyling, Marvel and Fatima who serve alongside me everyday in the field. Hope flows from each of you.

Thank you to Travis, Slate, Antonio, Devon and Meghan for being willing to entertain this thought and encourage its fruition.

Thank you to Taellor who is at the top of the totem pole forever.

This is in no way a reflection of me but rather a reflection of the One Who refuses to let us settle in this world. May He be glorified.

Forever more.

Forward

In 2004, we found ourselves in a place we could have never predicted. We found ourselves in a foreign mission field burying our only daughter. Throughout the journey in that valley, God showed us what true obedience looked like. He was ever faithful throughout that first year and continues to be so. As the devotions in 'Know Hope' came to an end, He was calling us deeper still.

We are a simple family, really. A husband, wife, four kids and a dog who have set out on a journey of obedience following God's call to serve as missionaries in Nicaragua. God called us here over ten years before the move would ever take place. Looking back, we know He was using that time to prepare us for what we would encounter here. We knew that our lives would forever be changed. We anticipated that our lives would never be the same again. However, we didn't foresee that it would forever change the landscape of our family. It did.

Through Taellor's death, we learned time and time again that sometimes it is sheer obedience that walks us through the journey that we have on this earth. We learned that joy can be found in any circumstances and the Hope is never elusive but rather resides in Our Father Who is continually with us. We learned that sometimes the walk is completed with tears falling and determination. We learned that His grace and mercies are new everyday just as the sun rises and sets. We became more of who were meant to be during this time. A tragedy that the world said should have destroyed us; He used it to flourish us.

Serving with Project H.O.P.E., we continue to have our dedicated ministries. Travis serves as a liaison to the short-term mission teams and Director of the base, myself as Director of Women's Ministry with the Center of Hope, a center for children living in a city dump community, Unshackled, a place of redemption and restoration for ladies in prostitution and extreme poverty, and the mothers at Taellor's House, a place that walks beside single moms providing a holistic care to the children and family as a whole.

We still believe that we are living the life that God has created us to live exactly where we were meant to be.

Our lives continue to be a walk of obedience. A desire to know Him more. A walk that continually changes, ebbing and flowing. A walk that isn't easy, yet is joyful. For those who read 'Know Hope', I pray that this book encourages you throughout your journey. I pray that it will challenge you in your faith.

You can read this as a book from cover to cover, jump around, and use it as a devotional or however God leads you to use it. There is a lot of empty space to allow for journaling and processing as you walk this journey of living worthy.

Praying for you as you walk amidst your journey through this world. May you find joy through simple obedience. You do not walk alone.

Tammy

Live Worthy

Family Structure | 1 Timothy 1:1-2

Paul, an apostle of Christ Jesus by the command of God our Savior and of Christ Jesus, our hope, To Timothy my true son in the faith: Grace, mercy and peace from God the Father and Christ Jesus our Lord.

Timothy and Paul had what today we would consider a unique relationship. Though outside of blood borne, Paul considered Timothy to be his true son in the faith. Through this relationship, Paul gives us an example of what it truly means to be sisters and brothers to our fellow believers. He demonstrates what it means to step outside of our worldly family borders and embrace others into our inner circle that we typical would consider reserved for family members only. Even those whom we only see on holidays, we don't speak to or that we may not even recognize them on a photo. Blood is thicker than water, yes?

But, maybe it is not. While God has placed us in a family and while God has given some of us our own family, maybe we were not meant to draw such distinct borders around such a personal family tree. Maybe we were created to be a part of a bigger picture perhaps a much bigger family tree. Quite possibly, we were designed to pour love, mercy and grace not only into our families but also into our family of believers.

In today's world, we find our families to be corralled, of sorts. This is my family. These are my kids. This is our home. This is our life. And then we dole out hastily written note cards, thrown-together casseroles, quick personal visits and even quicker prayers on behalf of our brothers and sisters in Christ because, frankly, there is little left over after we have served our own family.

And this is the part of the family that we love and cherish, but what about the other part of the family? The family part that is difficult. The family part that we know we have to love just because no matter what, no matter what, they are family. So we muster up what we have left and we try to create something that was never there to begin with and will never be.

And again, our Christian family receives the aftermath such as quick embraces at church, handshakes as we walk through the halls and, if we are lucky, one guiltily taken luncheon a year.

God has given us other Christian believers in which to walk this path of life with. He has surrounded each of us with "Paul's" and "Timothy's" as we journey through our path in this world.

Each of these relationships, when steeped firm in God's Word and love, can offer us the encouragement, accountability, intercessory prayer and true, true love that, quite frankly, will bring us to our knees in knowing that Our Father loves us so much that He sent us soldiers in this battle that we fight in this life. But we will never know it, we will never experience it, we will never even find it, if we don't look outside of our worldly-built lives beyond ourselves.

Does this mean we love our families less? Absolutely, not. This means we extend our inner circle. This means that we stop being superficial with those that we share our common faith and that we delve into each others lives Really delve. Not just for nosiness, not just for appearances but we truly start to purposefully walk this journey with our brothers and sisters in Christ. We hear of so many that are lonely, so many that are depressed and lacking encouragement while we all smile at each other and we benignly pass each other by. "But it might get messy." "I shouldn't get involved." "I don't have time to get involved."

It may mean a phone call at midnight that says "I need you" and you go. It will get messy and it is part of our obedience to our Heavenly Father to be involved and to walk together. Satan will hate it and will try everything in his power to forge up the walls of superficiality within our Christian circles. But we serve a Father that is more powerful than all.

Paul later would spend three years of his life in Ephesus with Timothy to serve the church alongside him. Three years. Who of our Christian faith do you know that would come and intimately walk with you?

For whom would you? It is so incredibly easy now to share our Christian journeys together. We have internet, phones, cars and planes! But, yet, we seem even more distant than maybe before. Separated.

Invest purposefully in whom God has sent you. Love them, cry with them, and be messy with them.

Who has God sent you to serve alongside?

What "messiness" do you continually avoid?

What specific action plan can you take today to live worthy?

Cunningly Crafted Diversion | 1 Timothy 1:3-4

As I urged you when I went into Macedonia, stay there in Ephesus so that you may command certain men not to teach false doctrines any longer nor to devote themselves to myths and endless genealogies. These promote controversies rather than God's work- which is by faith.

What better way is there to attract others, to attract attention or to gather a gathering? It doesn't even really matter the topic as long as there is some sort of drama attached to it and ears will turn your way and time will tick by. Useless information, much just speculation, yet, juicy enough to fill our minds and conversations. "She doesn't seem happy." "He's always at the office." "She's away from her family too much." "Their kids are just, well, different." As speculation swirls as to why each of these might be, we spend precious, precious time on imaginative words much as a child in imaginative play.

This is no less of an issue within the church. While God's Truth is actually quite simple. Salvation is offered, believed, repented and lived having the blessed assurance of eternal life while living in a loving relationship with Him while on this earth. Of course, the "devil is in the details", yes? And I am afraid that this is quite a literal statement when it comes to the seemingly "controversies" of faith. But how? But why? But who? Women or men? Or both? Where should we sit? How should we sit? Do we sing? Should we sing facing forward or backwards? Could we put the choir on the left side? Does it really matter? Yet, we spend time and time and more time debating these controversial topics within our church only stopping to dig into theology whilst trying to support our preferences or order to be right while creating committees and creating division.

Creating a diversion.

Yet, those are some of the simpler topics of controversy within our church.

Some would say that the real topics of controversy are found within the fine details such as baptisms for example: How to baptize, who can baptize, where to baptize? Baptize forwards or backwards. Or, what about the after life? I have been told more times than I can count, by well meaning Christians, myths and untruths concerning our daughter who resides in heaven at this very moment. Or, better yet, what about the Trinity? How does that really work? Hours and hours can be spent debating and discussing, sometimes arguing, trying to fill in the blanks.

And in this whole process, we are loosing precious time. Time that could be spent studying the Truth, studying God's word and listening for His Voice instead of our own.

Time that is literally instead spent on eternally irrelevant and worthless speculation. Time that could be spent reaching out to the lost is spent holed up discussing differences between believers. Between believers! While due to our seemingly need to be politically correct, we allow others who aren't believers to even come in and stir up the water, thinking that if we just find the right point, the right verse, the right answer, we can lead them to conversion.

Maybe sometimes we will. But what if, just maybe, this is all part of satan's work creating diversions and divisions within our churches and within our faith. God called us to be the peacemakers; yet, time and time again people have left the church broken-hearted and disillusioned. False teachers exist within our churches even today and I don't believe they are the ones sitting idle by. They are active in the quest to encourage as much controversy as possible and we allow it to happen. We take the bait and we go off on a tangent. We lose our focus.

It is not that the study of theology and God's Word is wrong but rather the mindless debate over speculated ideas may be placed just to occupy our focus away from what we have truthfully be called to do.

Choose today to live different. Not to fall for satan's ploy whether it be controversy over a current event, friend's life or God's Truth.

Don't feed into the chaos with speculation. Don't let our voice be the voice that muddies the water. Let's be the peacemakers reading our Bibles and spending time in prayer so that when the time comes and we encounter a false teacher we will know the falseness of their words and will not even enter into the debate of Truth. But rather, we will stand firm in our knowledge of Truth.

How firm is your belief in Truth?

Where might satan be creating a diversion in your life?

What specific action plan can you take today to live worthy?

Ours to Own | 1 Timothy 1:5

The goal of this command is love, which comes from a pure heart and a good conscious and a sincere faith.

And how do we love? We must have a pure heart. We must have a good conscious. We must have a sincere faith.

But what about that person that is making it so difficult for us to truly love them? Where does the responsibility lie with them? For it would be easy for us to genuinely love them if they would only make themselves lovable. If they would stop lying, if they would stop the dirty looks and malice attitude, then we would have no problem loving them.

But that's not how it works no matter how much we, ourselves, try to argue it to be. Nowhere here does it mention the other person. The commandment and the accountability to follow it lies at our feet and this is where it gets hard.

In today's world, we've got to stand up for ourselves. We've been taught and encouraged to always clear our name or that of our family. We have bought into the idea that 'ourselves' is more than anyone else. So, we can all get along as long as you follow certain rules and basic manners. But many times this doesn't even allow us to love the person but rather just to tolerate them for the sake of appearances, work relations or family dynamics.

The ability to love comes from within ourselves, within our own motives and hearts. It is ours alone to own. A discipline that each of us must develop in order to truly be able to extend love. Our only motivation must be to love not for our own personal gain but to simply love. It seems, though, that in our world today, we have even lost what love is.

Remember, love is patient, kind, doesn't envy or boast, is not proud, rude or self-seeking. Love is not easily angered, keeps no records of wrong, does not delight in evil but rejoices in truth. Love always protects, trusts, always hopes and perseveres.

Love never fails.

But that is all impossible for us to do, yes? For if others only could see all of the faults that we see in the other person, then all would understand that our inability to love them is completely justified.

But, yet, the ability to love isn't built through anyone else but rather through ourselves. So if we find ourselves impatient, unkind, boastful or proud.

If we are rude, look out for our own interests above all else or have a temper that is easily provoked, we do not represent love. If we can list every wrong that anyone has ever committed against us, while all the while patting ourselves on the back for being able to still speak to them, we do not point others towards love. When we find ourselves delighting in evil and neglecting the Truth, as we become less protective, less trusting, less hopeful and with the inability to persevere, we are not obeying His command. When we look around and we see failure not in ourselves but all around us, we must search ourselves. Honestly.

Live Worthy

Christ, personally, lived and walked among those that by all accounts were unbelievably unkind to Him. Yet when He hung from the cross, He did not read a list of names identifying those that because of their bad actions were exempt from His death. He died for all of us. Each and every one. He gave us an example. An example not just in how we should love but an example of how one with a pure heart must live while in, yet set apart from this world.

He lived with a good conscious even when wronged. He is the ultimate peacemaker. He demonstrated pure faith to the Father through prayer and praise never once pointing to Himself.

It is a choice that begins and ends with us. We can't do it alone. We have to let Him love through us but, first, we must be a willing vessel desiring above all else to live a life that is truly worth living. For the goal of all of this, each and every bit is love.

What is your definition of love as demonstrated by your actions?

Who do you struggle to demonstrate love towards?

What specific action plan can you take today to live worthy?

Meaningless Talk | 1 Timothy 1:6

Some have wandered away from these and turned to meaningless talk.

Meaningless talk.

Referring to false teachers, Paul reminds us that there are those that will spend huge amounts of time focusing on minuscule details in the Bible arguing and debating minor points of sheer conjuncture to the exclusion of the main point of the whole thing. Wasting time focusing on things that are truthfully of no relevance.

But doesn't this apply to ourselves, also. How much time do we waste in the details, arguing and replaying, sometimes only in our own minds, instead of just doing what God has asked us to do. Every day things, even going to church for example, turn into a dialogue about us instead of about Him. "What should I wear?" "Are the kids dressed?" " Where are their shoes?" "Where will we eat afterwards?" Or "Should we even go today?" All valid points but do we combine them with God?

Or for example, Christmas. Is God at the center, or simply an after thought tacked onto a whirlwind of a holiday? As we rush off to this party and that party, as we give and receive gifts, as we bake and eat massive meals, how often do we speak of Him? How many of these gatherings do we bow our heads in prayer offering true praise? How many of our gatherings are fellowshipping in His Name?

How often have we simply just sat in His presence being still?

Pure hearts, good conscious and sincere faith doesn't come by accident. They aren't a given added into our lives. We must be purposeful and disciplined seeking first Him.

It means setting ourselves apart from the holiday frenzy and focusing sincerely on the holiday. Festivities are fun and should be enjoyed but when festivities are the bulk of our holiday, is not our actions meaningless?

So, then we debate. Well, maybe the date, actual date of Christmas Day wasn't the actual day, maybe the wise men didn't see a baby but rather a young boy or maybe, Mary was holding the baby instead of Him lying in a manger? Or was there even a manger present? And on and on it goes with the devil in the details, literally.

Be still today. Be still this next Christmas. It's not too late. For this all will end, and when that time comes the gifts won't matter, the tree, the food, the clothes but what will matter will be where eternity will be spent for those that God has placed in our world each and every one.

How is Christ at the forefront of your activities that you have planned today?

If others were observing your day-to-day life, would they see God as the main event or simply an afterthought?

What specific action plan can you take today to live worthy?

Baffled | 1 Timothy 1:7

They want to be teachers of the law, but they do not know what they are talking about or what they so confidently affirm.

This one baffles me.

Paul, again, is referring to false teachers. Teachers who want to teach God's Word even though they just don't get it. They profess vehemently with their mouths, pledge their devotion and garner many followers, yet they have not a clue what they are really teaching.

I think that when we hear the words false teacher our mind conjectures images of hapless speakers, well-spoken salesmen and other easily identifiable, therefore, easily dismissible characters. However much as the evil in this world masquerades as all shiny and smooth, so do those who speak falsely regarding God's Word.

They speak easily of His faithfulness. They speak eloquently of His love and forgiveness; yet, they themselves have not a clue as to the realness of the Words they speak. With charisma that would lull the depths of complacency into action, they quickly gather devoted followers and supporters. As they impart His Word to those that gather, they are quick to hold all at arms bay not too get to involved, too deep or too real. Much like the Wizard of Oz, one great big show, pleasing to the eyes and impactful to the senses but a fraud, nonetheless.

And this is where I become baffled. Do they really know so little of God's Word that they don't get that this is real? I mean as in the parting of the seas, turning water into wine, plagues and eternal judgment real! This isn't some easily forgotten hoax or quick buck to be made sort of deal. This is real. They play on a playing ground that goes way beyond their spiritual depth.

And then I realize, that they really do not know.

They have been deceived by the greatest of deceptors. They've been shown a way to live that involves sharing God's Word without really ever living it. They've been played and they have bought it hook, line and sinker. And as with any sin, it starts off small and works to envelope our all life leading us to the road of destruction, as does this one.

I now look upon teachers of God's Word differently. I look past the smoothness or the polish on their presented Words and look at their lives. Is there fruit or are they surrounded by legalistic borders? Do they share stories and real-life encounters that are really real? Do they exude the love of Christ and show it in their daily walk?

I've met my fair share of false teachers and by some, I've been initially blindsided then I was speechless for to see the curtain pulled back and to see "the show" instead of Truth hurt. Yet, we are warned time and time again that they exist and they do.

For those of us that teach, fair warning. Don't just teach to fill a slot or to gain worldly favor for to teach God's Word comes with great responsibility and with it great persecution from satan. Don't take the responsibility lightly or with pride. It is an honor and privilege.

God's Word, whether your wish to partake or not, is real. You can amass worldly gains from it but the eternal ramifications will be costly.

What fruit can be observed as a result of your obedience to the King?

How do you respond to false teachers?

What specific action plan can you take today to live worthy?

The Law | 1 Timothy 1:8

We know that the law is good if one uses it properly.

The law. A list of dos and don'ts. Mandates. Rules and regulations.

In this world, we look upon them as a giant chasm between us and God. Added with satan's lies which quickly point out that the list is far to long and hefty, we know that we will never get to the other side with each rule separating us from whom our very soul yearns. We look at our current lives against the backdrop of the law and we are quickly discouraged at the distance we assume we must cover.

We look at ourselves compared to those that are seemingly able to keep the law. There they go with their perfect marriages, perfect children, lives and jobs. They must have something that we don't have. They had parents that loved and supported them. They had the perfect schooling and friends and grew up on the right side of town and sit in the right pew at church. They live blessed and easy lives that encourage them to follow the law. Yes?

Or maybe we try. We try to follow the law and do make some progress. We attend church long enough for the ushers to greet us by name and the pastor to recognize our face. Maybe we even commit to serve, hoping this will help our chasm to shorten. We stop watching questionable movies and partaking of things in excess and we feel our chests swell as we look back and see what we have done only to look ahead and see that this chasm is just as wide and deep as it was before. We are no closer than we were when we started and no one has even noticed. Not one single person. So, we stop. Discouraged and betrayed, we stop.

The law was never meant to be a chasm between us and God that we scale alone. It was meant to be a journey that we walk with Him step by step. The moment when we look at that chasm and say, "No way can I do this alone.

But God, I trust You and You alone to walk me through this." This is the moment when we realize that it is all about Him and not us. It is all about Him and not the law.

We, at that moment, will not seek to obey the law out of necessity but rather out of love and desire to be in His presence. We find that the laws are no longer a prison of dos and don'ts but rather freedom from the trappings of this world; freedom that we will only find in Christ.

As the old hymn says, "Come just as you are". Come. He awaits. The world will try to ravel this to be the greatest mystery of all and, yet, this, above all things, is what we have been created for.

This is our destiny.

How big does the "chasm" seem between you and God at this moment?

Where might you be trying to earn your way to a relationship with Him instead of pursuing one?

What specific action plan can you take today to live worthy?

No Middle Ground | 1 Timothy 1:9-11

We also know that law is made not for the righteous but for the lawbreakers and rebels, the ungodly and sinful, the unholy and irreligious; for those that kill their father or mothers, for murderers, for adulterers and perverts, for slave traders and liars and perjurers- and for whatever else is contrary to the sound doctrine that conforms to the glorious gospel of the blessed God, which He entrusted to me.

No ifs, no maybes, no sometimes but sound doctrine. It either is or it isn't. No middle ground. No room for political correctness or does everyone win. Sound doctrine. Only.

We've moved into a worldview that everyone, as long as they have good intentions, could be right. We live in a society that rejects black and white yet embraces many shades of gray (literally). Anything goes and if it doesn't; then shame on the one who stops it. We base our actions on the measuring stick of the world instead of from the Word.

And there is a difference.

The world says our human desires whatever they might be should be fulfilled no matter the cost. The world says that we deserve to be happy, for we have earned it no matter the cost. The world says that we are the ruler of our world no matter the cost. As long as we follow the rules of the land, we can be the master of our own domain. We are in control and it simply doesn't matter who gets hurt in the process or aftermath.

But, we are not worthy of any of that. ==We fall under an authority that is far greater than any authority in this world.== It is an authority that varies greatly from this world being the authority of the Most High. From His grace, we find ourselves in a much different position than the world has pitched to us. We find that "the last is first and the first is last" mentality.

We are told that the meek will inherit the earth not the last man standing, but the meek. Blessed are the poor in spirit and those who mourn, the merciful, pure in heart and the peacemakers.

And blessed are those who hunger and thirst for righteousness or are even persecuted for it for they will be fulfilled and will find that theirs is the kingdoms of heaven. From the Sermon on the Mount, Jesus reveals not how it should be but how it is.

This is how it is. It doesn't matter if we choose to partake or not, doesn't matter if we affirm or not this is how it is. And ==for those that are believers, this is not a game of multiple choice where we can choose to abide by a few and neglect the rest.==

This is the total package.

A package that is in direct opposition to what this world dangles in front of us. Direct opposition from what satan's lies would spin. Direct opposition to what our fleshy human desires would seek. Yet, perfectly aligned with our soul. Perfectly aligned with that part of us that will never die whether in heaven or hell. That part. The part of us that will never find true joy or peace until we are perfectly aligned with Him.

Live Worthy

==In a world of gray, there is Truth always,== there is Truth.

How does the world continue to influence your desires?

Where might satan be spinning lies in your life?

What specific action plan can you take today to live worthy?

Privilege | 1 Timothy 1:12

I thank Christ Jesus our Lord, who has given me strength, that He considered me faithful, appointing me to His service.

Have we forgotten the privilege?

We toil our days away. Quickly, one day blends into the next. Day after day as if they were endless.

We serve half-heartedly. Initially with enthusiasm that quickly wanes to disgruntled obligation, we put in our time. We serve in our slot counting down the minutes and seconds for the appointed time to end. Hoping the sermon today isn't a long one while satan weaves lies that we have been taken advantage of yet again as we serve in the area He has placed us to serve.

Or, maybe we hide in the sea of blurred faces and live always waiting for someone to reach out to us, yet, always staying just beyond reach. Trying not to get involved, yet, yearning to be involved. And as we watch, we observe others being where we want to be, with friendships that we long to have and satan reminds us that we are not worthy. He reminds us that we have been given a front row seat in observation only.

Have we forgotten? Our strength, our favor comes from Him and Him alone. He has seen our faithfulness and has appointed us, yes us, to His service. We personally have an appointment from the Most High. What an honor.

An appointment that comes from He who is all-knowing. He who sees the purpose of where He has placed us even when we do not. In a world that focuses on titles, accomplishments and notoriety, we have been placed in position by the One who sees what is most important. Eternal value.

So that sobbing preschooler, that needy neighbor, that annoying person standing beside you (working with you, talking to you, living with you). Perhaps, you have been placed there for a reason, for a purposeful reason. Instead of looking at each of our encounters with people as opportunities to enrich our lives, we need to look past ourselves and see what we can do to enrich theirs.

How can we serve Him instead of waiting for ourselves to be served?

It's not easy. It is a completely different mindset than most of us have been taught, observed and lived but it is a privilege not to be taken lightly nor exploited but rather cherished.

Who in your life have you been labeling as annoying when in actuality, they may be an opportunity to serve God?

Who do you find yourself avoiding?

What specific action plan can you take today to live worthy?

Once Was | 1 Timothy 1:13

Even though I was once a blasphemer and a persecuted and a violent man, I was shown mercy because I acted in ignorance and unbelief.

Was once but am no more.

Oh how I love Paul's story. A story of such redemption. A story of a man so totally sold out for what he believed to be truth that he dismissed and criticized the actual Truth. He was so loyal to his cause that he persecuted and killed for it. He thought he was doing rightful work and he did it with all he had. He sought and killed Christians. Until the day that God revealed to him the Truth, and on that day, he was humble enough to accept that he had been dreadfully wrong and changed.

Now, we aren't talking about a simple disagreement, misunderstanding wrong or a few hurt feelings and dirty looks wrong. We are talking about an entire career, an entire life-cause wrong. Paul's life mission at that time was to rid the earth of all Christians by whatever means necessary. He wasn't even Paul yet but rather was known by Saul who was a man greatly feared by all Jews.

Until that fateful day, God literally blinded him. Saul had an encounter with the One True God that day. An encounter that immediately changed his life. An encounter that he chose to embrace.

And this is what I love about Paul.

He immediately recognized the error of his ways and changed radically. He turned away from his current position of both notoriety and stature and became just as sold out for converting for Christianity as he had just days before killing them.

When he came face to face with Truth, he aligned himself with Truth even if it meant publicly acknowledging his whole life up until that point was a lie. He changed even though it meant alienating himself from those who revered him and joining those who feared him. He stepped out alone.

However in his heart, that didn't seem to matter. What mattered was his allegiance to the Truth. It didn't matter that he might be publicly scorned, what his friends would think, "how he could save face" or "how it could be spun to make it politically acceptable". What mattered was simply the Truth, no matter the cost.

May we all be so humble that when encountered with Truth we instantly align ourselves with Him. We don't look left or right. We don't see how it will "fit" in this world nor the cost but we choose Him. May we not ever be so proud that we stumble over the wrongness of our ways.

Where in your life are you simply wrong?

How can you be like Paul and make an about face?

What specific action plan can you take today to live worthy?

Abundantly | 1 Timothy 1:14

The grace of our Lord was poured out on me abundantly, along with the faith and love that are in Christ Jesus.

Imagine being quite possibly the man that Christians feared most in this world. Imagine martyring instead of being martyred. This was Paul's life prior to his encounter with God. This was Paul's life as Saul. The one most feared, the one most hated and the one most intent on wiping out every morsel of Christianity.

Yet when God revealed the Truth, Paul immediately changed and the Lord poured out His grace abundantly.

With the change of Paul's heart, God not just extended forgiveness and mercy but poured out His grace abundantly. Grace not in measured increments consistent with his time of "remorsefulness " but grace extended abundantly.

Abundantly. And, yet, there are many of us who couldn't accept God's abundant flow of grace in our lives if it slapped us in the face and sometimes it does! We journey through this world holding ourselves accountable to past issues when everyone else has forgotten. We limp through our lives tethered to past sins that have long been forgiven but in our mind not forgotten. We carry, gathered in our arms, a past that causes our heads to fall in shame missing completely on the abundant fall of His grace in our lives.

I'm not taking about living a life flippantly or carelessly but rather a life filled with abundant grace knowing that the same God that poured abundant grace over Paul's life is the same God that pours abundant grace our life.

Grace. Abundantly.

What would our lives look like if we lived in the grace that has been poured upon us? If we embraced every single drop of love that He extends? Imagine a life well steeped in abundant grace from top to bottom. Satan doesn't want us to find that place.

The moment in our lives where our life is so changed that we go from being a "Saul" to a "Paul", the moment when we realize what grace really means instead of the watered down version that many of us survive in teetering back and forth from one abyss to another never firmly planting our feet on His firm foundation is the moment when true freedom is found.

No sin is too big, no past too brazen. Let's start living today in His abundant grace. We say we believe, we know the Truth but many of us still live as if tethered to our old selves. Find freedom in Him.

Where in your life are you staying tethered to past sins?

How can you be like Paul and accept God's abundant grace?

What specific action plan can you take today to live worthy?

He > I | 1 Timothy 1:15

Here is a trustworthy saying that deserves full acceptance: Christ Jesus came into the world to save sinners-of whom I am the worst.

He came to save us.

He came to save us from ourselves, to save us from a faltering world, to save us from an eternity separated from Him. He came so we could be and be abundantly.

And we know this, we read the words, we've said the prayer. We share it with the world. But when the world looks into our lives, do they see that we believe this with everything that we are? Do they see a life forgiven? A life that says, "He came for me."

We spend a lot of time in our lives searching for recognition from this world. We spend a lot of time in our lives searching for a seal of approval from others. We spend a lot of time in our lives searching for a seal that may never be forthcoming. We alter who we are and what we do to make others happy. Adjusting our life to make way for their needs because isn't that what a Christian should do?

Make others happy?

So we delve deeper into the world, into relationships trying to make happiness abound, yet, when we look around it seems like there is a never ending pit of insecurities that we have just taken on as our own personal cause and no one is happy. At which point we typically go one of two ways. We either get our feelings hurt and walk away with our hearts hardening or we dig deeper determined to fix their world.

Because that is what we do.

Or do we? How many times do we actually find happiness in God's Word? Yes, there is happiness but is it found abundantly?

Is it the resounding theme throughout? If we were to summarize the Bible, would the word happy even be a part of our summary? Did Christ come so we could be happy every single day of our lives?

And, yet, we strive to find that happy place overlooking the very One who can give us peace amongst the storm. While distracted by satan's ploys we many times try to satisfy those around us with more of ourselves, when what they really need is more of Him, not more of me, not more of you, but more of the only one that can quench their thirst.

I've walked this path. I've tried to bring happiness and joy and I have failed miserably. Miserably. In fact, I think there was less happiness when I tried than when I didn't and, yet, I kept trying to fill a hole I was never meant to fill that I would never be able to fill. I came to realize that if I were able to fill that need, to fill that void and need then they would never search for Him. In my quest to "save them", I was keeping them from the very One that could actually save them.

It's a fine line, yes? The dance of shining Christ's Light instead of showcasing our own show. A line that can only be walked when we stay close to Him who has saved us. It is a walk that is done with complete and utter humility. It is a walk that is not of our own doing.

More of Him and less of me.

Who are you discouraging from turning to God?

Where do you need to step aside and let God work?

What specific action plan can you take today to live worthy?

The Worst of Sinners | 1 Timothy 1:16

But for that very reason I was shown mercy so that in me, the worst of sinners, Christ Jesus might display his unlimited patience as an example for those who would believe on him and receive eternal life.

The worst of sinners.

Not one of the worst, not some of the worst but THE worst of sinners. This letter is thought to have been written by Paul to Timothy just prior to Paul's final imprisonment. Many moons had passed over his history as being Saul. He was now a revered teacher of God's Word. He was sought after by those who he had once served alongside. He brought the Truth to the gentiles and he, himself, was a prime example of true transformation.

And, yet, he still referred to himself as being the worst of sinners. He never forgot. He walked with humility also in remembrance that it was by Christ's grace he had been saved. By Christ and Christ alone, he was a changed man. He never adopted the attitude that we see so often in our religious circles today. An attitude that forgets what each one of us once was, a sinner destined for hell. An attitude that projects itself as holier than.

But holier than what? Than others? Than Christ, himself?

We all strive to walk a path in obedience to our Father. It is an individual path that, thankfully, we have been granted the sweetness of fellowship with other believers to share in our journey. But with lies and twisted agendas, satan has taken what should be encouragement and turned it many times into a place where we are uncomfortable to share areas where we struggle, places where we are simply inept or the valleys of our life.

We share the mountaintop experiences over and over. Sometimes we share the same one for years and years clinging to that moment when we experienced God while privately grieving our personal despair of trying to find Him now.

And as each of us take on this persona, those who are seeking often times see a group of people that are seemingly perfect, maybe even too perfect for themselves. We create an illusion that all is well.

I overheard a conversation once between one of the poorest of the poor in the city dump and a person from America. The lady who lived in the dump had been asked how a church body back home might could pray for her. And after sharing her prayer requests, she looked up in the eyes of the one who asked and said, "And how might I pray for you?"

To which the person from America quickly replied, "I have everything I need. I don't need prayers like you need them."

Don't we? Sure if you are reading this, you are in the top wealthy of the world even if at times it doesn't seem like it. If you ate today at least one meal, consider yourself lucky. If you have a vehicle at your disposal to drive, can read and a house, you are one of the most fortunate but are you? See, we spend a lot of our time and resources looking at the wealthy and the poor but we use measures of materialism. I have lots of things that must mean I am fine.

But am I?

What about my spiritual depth? Do I really know Christ? Isn't that what really matters when everything is finished here? My house, my car, my bank account, my, my, my. None of that will matter when my last breath on this earth is taken. So how am I really? Have I accepted Him as my Savior or do I use my busy life as an excuse to believe but not really believe.

I think through Paul, we see a heart totally sold out to God and out of that we see humility. We see someone willing to share their past with others that are seeking, not to brag or boast but to share the vastness of God's grace.

I once was that but through His grace and power I am no more. We aren't afraid of the realness of life, the messiness and the craziness. We realize that we are safe and secure in our God's hands and that is all that matters.

Where do you find your identity?

How can you be like Paul and be a giant of the faith and yet the most humble of all?

What specific action plan can you take today to live worthy?

What Do We Know | 1 Timothy 1:17

Now to the King eternal, immortal, invisible, the only God, be honor and glory forever and ever. Amen.

Can we really read this standing or sitting so informally?

Or do we read this with the same cavalier attitude in which we read the morning's headlines? Do we listen to these words in the same manner that we hear the news? Do we behold these words in the same reverence as our favorite novel, magazine or schoolbook? Or, God forgive us, with less than?

Eternal. Immortal. Invincibile.

It seems that we want to experience and be witness to His power when we are in need. We yearn to see Him move mountains and rain His provisions but do we understand? Do we really understand His magnitude?

If we did, would we choose to go about our days differently? Would we live lives that tend to things more eternal instead of plastics and woods? Would we stand more assuredly with shoulders straight and heads bowed in humbleness. We serve a mighty King.

We seem to live in a strange balance between being prideful of our religion and, yet, being timid when we come face to face to the evilness. We seem to sway just off of center instead of firmly planted on His foundation.

Do we really not know who He is?

And if we do, do our lives reflect His vast greatness?

He is the great I Am. The same God of Abraham, David and Joseph.

And in this, we should sleep soundly. We should work steadfastly. We should honor greatly with every fiber of our being.

I thought I knew of His greatness and power until our daughter passed away. That day, I stood in sheer awe of His Magnitude. His power. His reach. Who He is. It was like I had pulled back the curtain expecting to find despair and the "Wizard of Oz" turned out to be even greater than He had shown me before.

I came to experience God in His glory but at the same time in His compassion in His justness and in His gentleness.

Who would have thought that what are contradictions in this world could coexist together.

Such is the God we serve.

What do you truly know of His Holiness?

How does your life reflect His Magnitude?

What specific action plan can you take today to live worthy?

The Fight | 1 Timothy 1:18-19

Timothy, my son, I give you this instruction in keeping with the prophecies once made about you, so that by following them you may fight the good fight, holding on to faith and a good conscious.

Conjures up images of battle grounds and weapons or maybe a backyard brawl with fists swinging and bloodied lips and noses or even perhaps a name calling screaming tangle of bodies.

A fight in the physical realm.

Oftentimes we forget the fights that occur in the spiritual realm. The battles that we fight every day against the evilness in this world are such a part of our lives that we simple forget that they are in constant opposition of our very souls and we begin to simply accept the oppression we feel as simply the life we've been allotted.

A life that is difficult, hard and without much color. A life that drags itself out of bed in the morning, makes itself presentable to the world while internally counting the moments until it can fall back into slumber. Or maybe it is a life that is so filled with worry and despair that sleep is evasive and nights are spent in tortured silence as the world calms and the voices of doubt and despair creep in.

And we accept this simply as the cards that we have been dealt and the battle rages on.

Whether we wish to believe or not, there is a spiritual realm that seeks to destroy. It's every intent is to make your outlook on your life to be miserable, hated, dreadful and everything opposite to what Christ would offer. It seeks to put us into such a tailspin that we even start to doubt what true joy is and just maybe we didn't even know what it was to begin with.

Such is the good fight.

A fight against good and evil. A fight that would pit us against those who seek to discredit us. A fight that would harden our hearts and create disillusion in our minds. A fight that would leave us heartbroken and betrayed. Stooped if not broken.

We try to reach out to others only to grasp no one failing to realize that they themselves are simply trying to just survive. We try to comfort ourselves with money, love, food and a whole slew of earthly offering only to find ourselves in further bondage than we were to begin with.

And then we remember.

Christ.

He offered to carry our burdens. He offered to lighten our load and through faith in Him we find hope. We find discernment to recognize the heaviness for what it truly is. We find the strength and grace to breathe when the battles get too heavy. We learn, by His mercy, we can choose a life of joy even in insurmountable circumstances and then we learn that we can quickly see the darkness for what it truly is; simply a weighted mystic that darkens this world yet has no bearing on our souls.

While we serve the God of Abraham, David and Joseph, we also walk amongst the same evils that they encountered.

Stand ready.

What are you battling in your everyday life?

How often do you don the armor of God?

What specific action plan can you take today to live worthy?

Shipwrecked | 1 Timothy 1:19

Some have rejected these and so have shipwrecked their faith.

Some will reject a good conscious. It comes with free will. A choice. Do I choose to listen to the innermost whisper in my being or do I choose to ignore it and blaze my own path?

The innermost whispers of God, at first, surprised me. Reminded me of when I first felt my firstborn move inside me. Did I really feel something? Was that more than my own flesh and blood moving? As he grew stronger and as I became more attuned to his movements, I learned to identify his movements assuredly. No longer did I question what I knew to be happening. I knew that I knew.

Such as been my walk with God. The urging from my conscious trying to guide me in the path I should go. I learned to listen. It is more than just simple thoughts or ideas but guidance from the Father as He speaks to me.

Sometimes, it seems very strong such as a desire to just sit still or to go and do. Turn left. Turn right. And sometimes, it is merely knowing that I am enveloped in His will. Sometimes, it is just simply knowing that this path is the correct path.

But the strongest directive is when I face the possibility of walking outside of His will. When I encounter the darkness in this world, it seems as if my conscious comes alive reminding me again and again that this is the wrong path, the wrong way.

Though it may sound alarms within my body, I can override its direction and choose my own path. I can choose to do wrong. I can choose not to listen.

And as I choose not to listen, my discernment seems to be less astute seeming to be less in tune with the Truth.

So that the next time, I can choose the wrong path with less distraction from my conscious and less interference from my Father and I begin a journey walking apart from He who loves me.

As the journey continues, my conscious that once was strong and loud has dwindled to merely being a bystander as my ship starts to flounder.

One drink doesn't hurt. This movie isn't so bad. One look is okay. As long as we just talk, everything is fine. I can roll my eyes at him behind his back and still be submissive.

And all of a sudden we find ourselves in a direction opposite with those who we know have our best interests in mind. We distance ourselves from them because they just don't understand and once again, we override our conscious to do what we want to do.

Before we know it, we have fallen into satan's snare and we are pleading to hear God's voice once again. We falter when we realize that the snare is actually prettier on the outside than we could have ever imagined. We had envisioned his snare to be one of murder and such when in reality we find ourselves in some of his most common snares of dishonesty and deceit. The web was spun and we stayed when we should have ran and the pretty walls begin to fall revealing the ugliness in its path.

If we only would have listened.

Pray. Stay close to Him. When doubt clouds our view, we must run (not walk) to where we experienced Him last.

What beauty are you experiencing that is actually a mirage of sin?

How can you prepare yourself to hear His voice?

What specific action plan can you take today to live worthy?

Stand Firm | 1 Timothy 1:20

Among them are Hymenaeus and Alexander, whom I have handed over to Satan to be taught not to blaspheme.

What a life lesson to be handed over to satan in order to be taught a lesson.

We can be as obstinate as we choose. Touting free will and freedom of choice or we can spout of a list a mile long of wrongs that we have endured which is why we have chosen the path on which we find ourselves.

It simply doesn't matter.

There is an end that many paths descend upon. It is a path riddled with excuses and betrayals. A path upon which many people have traveled seeking something. The ever elusive something.

Whether it be fame, fortune, love or any one of the long lists of wants and desires. Any of these can be sought and used for good or can be idolized and used for bad. The focus is what is deep in our heart. What are our motives? Do we seek for ourselves or for the good of the kingdom or worse do we seek for the kingdom and use for ourselves. Seeking that something.

And by seeking that 'something' we lose everything.

The saddest twist of all is that three words could have saved it all, "Help me Jesus."

We walk in a world with an enemy that seeks to destroy but we, also, walk in a world with a Savior that has conquered it all. Believe in Him fully. Walk carefully. Stand firm.

What are you seeking today?

What are your true motives?

What specific action plan can you take today to live worthy?

Power Of Prayer | 1 Timothy 2:1-2

I urge then, first of all, that requests, prayers, intercession and thanksgiving be made for everyone-for kings and all those in authority, that we may live peaceful and quiet lives in all godliness and holiness.

Prayer when we eat, prayer when we sleep and prayer when we need. All focusing on we, we, we. Ourselves.

How often, truthfully, do we pray for everyone? Kings, queens, all authority figures. Everyone. Or do we pray simply for those that are connected in some manner to those who interconnect into our lives.

Now let's put aside royalty, how often are we on our knees for those we love? How often do we bow our heads for those we know? How many words have we raised on those of whom we greatly hate? Or worse, how many prayers have we not prayed when we said that we would.

"I'm praying for you."

I pray that there is not an account of how many times we say this and simply forget.

This list of people would be massive if we really did this. We would have people on our list from the farthest king to the closest of our loves and everyone in between. We would pray a lot.

But maybe that is what we are truly meant to do. Pray a lot. We are instructed to pray without ceasing perhaps this is why.

Maybe we have made prayer something more than it is supposed to be or is that less than?

We've created prayer journals, prayer closets, prayer reminders, prayer altars and prayer benches and, yet, do we pray more? Or do we confine ourselves to only pray at these times in these moments.

We are to pray without ceasing. Just as we breathe without ceasing, we should be in prayer. To cease breathing is to cease living. To cease praying engages us in a battle that we will be ill prepared for and ill equipped to withstand. And yes, He already knows. But somehow, someway having those words pass through our lips helps to align our thoughts with His. We find ourselves less me-focused and more Kingdom focused. We find ourselves less worldly focused and more eternal focused.

We find ourselves in communion with the King without even trying. Satan will try to convince us that it takes a program, a place, a special person or chair to pray. He will do anything he can to stop our direct communication with our Father, which should be the simplest of all things.

Don't miss such a gift. Don't get too busily caught up on things to miss out on daily walking with Him.

Whom did you pray for yesterday?

Whom did you not pray for yesterday?

What specific action plan can you take today to live worthy?

All | 1 Timothy 2:3-4

This is good, and it pleases God our Savior, who wants all men to be saved and to come to a knowledge of the Truth.

Not one. Not some but all.

This seems to be a difficult concept for us. Perhaps, the perplexity comes from genuinely realizing the vastness of Our Father's knowledge. He is all knowing with no hindrance of time. He knows before the question is asked what the answer will be. He knows before the day even begins how it will set a day a hundred years from now. He's the only One who knows when the last day will set for each of us and for this world, as we know it.

We simply can't fathom this knowledge and since we can't wrap our minds completely around it we struggle with it. Satan seeks this opportunity to cast doubt in our minds regarding the Truth. This combined with our tendency to see people through our eyes instead of God's makes for a dangerous combination.

We start to pick and choose.

There are some people that we really, really, really want to accept Christ. We invite them to every special program the church has during which we pray constantly in our minds that they will hear and receive the Truth all the while flinching if something is said that we think might offend them. Sometimes, we even bargain for their souls. "God, if you would only do this then I will _____." We grace their lives with books and Bibles trying to find just the right combination that will open their eyes.

And then there are those that we don't. It's not that we don't want them to receive Christ. They just aren't on our radar.

Our hearts aren't intertwined with theirs for whatever reason. We cross their paths every single day yet not once do we question their destination for eternity. We simply don't want to get involved. Someone else can.

Or, what about those that we have written off. Those that we have already judged in our hearts and minds that should spend eternity in hell beginning today. Sometimes, we mean this cavalierly. They've wronged us and we are just truly apathetic towards them. While sometimes, the evilness that lurks within is greater and there is no question where our judgment lies.

But, God wants all men.

As we continue to seek His will in all of our ways, we will find that some of the lines of our life will begin to blur. Divisions that our human minds have created will begin to fade. This is His work not ours. He allows us to be a part, a small part. Our part is to simply be obedient to Him and whatever that entails. Perhaps we will find that it isn't only our invitations to special church events that save our friends and family but our everyday walk that sets us apart. It will be when our lives are scented with a peace and calmness in this chaotic world when they will see something that they want to be a part of. If our Christian lives reflect more and more of this world, then there is no reason why they should look deeper. It appears, on the outside anyway, that there is no difference.

None.

We have marriages that seem to be failing just as much inside the church as outside. We have pornography, hypocrisy and lies that run deep in our church bodies. Depression, hatred and gossip walking the very church walls that are holding signs promising abundant joy.

We must fight this fight head-on. Do we really believe what we believe? If we do, then satan gets no more of this. We are reclaiming the abundant joy that God has called us to have. To do that will require an obedience and discipline that this world seems to have forgotten but in which our very souls crave. Sometimes it is just hard work.

Live different. Live worthy.

Whom do you beg God to bring into His fold?

Whom would you rather not be given freedom through grace and mercy?

What specific action plan can you take today to live worthy?

No one. | 1 Timothy 2:5-6

For there is one God and one mediator between God and men, the man Christ Jesus, who gave himself as a ransom for all men- the testimony given in its proper time.

And with this comes freedom.

Within each of us is the power to come before the Father and pray. This doesn't require a special building or a special person to appeal to the Father on our behalf. No one's prayer is more or less important than the next and no one's prayer is more or less powerful than the next.

Regardless of title.

No one.

We've bestowed upon ourselves a multitude of titles. Titles to distinguish ourselves. While the positions with the titles were meant to be ones of service to God's people, the world seems to have twisted them into something more.

Positions of power.

And with positions of power come many things; areas within our lives that brings about pride and greed. We begin to think about ourselves as being more than or maybe just sat even farther apart from the world than our fellow Christians.

Live Worthy

Jesus, in Luke, told us a parable about the Great Samaritan. Injured and laying on the side of the road, he was passed by two men of the church. They each saw him and for whatever reason they continued on without helping.

Maybe they were late to something? Maybe they thought it would get too messy? Hopefully, they didn't think it was beneath them.

Or possibly they realized that no one was there to see their response so they continued on forgetting that there is always someone watching even when we are alone on this earth.

For even when man doesn't see, our Father does.

Within each of us, regardless of our stature in this lot of life, hold the privilege to come before Him, to serve Him and to be His in this world. It doesn't take a special ceremony or special effects, but rather a pure heart and motives.

We must seek Him and only Him.

What worldly titles do you hold?

Which title would those who know you bestow upon you first?

What specific action plan can you take today to live worthy?

True Center | 1 Timothy 2:7

And for this purpose I was appointed a herald and an apostle--I am telling the truth, I am not lying--and a teacher of the true faith to the Gentiles.

A statement of truth.

Even Paul was accused of lying. Even, Paul had to say, "I am telling the truth, I am not lying."

And, yet, there would be those who would continue to believe, no matter what evidence that Paul could lay before them, that he was not being truthful. Paul didn't even believe the Truth until God opened His eyes. Prior to that day, he would have been siding vehemently with his own opposition.

So how do we find our true center while living amidst a world swirling in opinions and commentary, critics and acclaimers, encouragers and naysayers?

Truth is found at the foundation of our beliefs. Paul placed his belief on the firm foundation of Christ. A foundation that never sways, changes or distorts. The same yesterday, today and tomorrow. Truth.

And this is our center. This is where we begin and end. There is no deviation.

There will be those who say things that are not true about us. There will be mockers and critics. Our own family members may disown or try to discredit us but our foundation of Truth never changes.

And within a foundation of Truth that never changes we find peace in knowing that in spite of worldly debates we can stand upon a Truth that doesn't waver. One bit.

This is also how we will find joy when the world can't find it. We place our contentment not on things of this world for they will ebb and flow but rather on things eternal that will withstand the test of time.

When we place our sights above what will fall from our human grasp, we find that the trappings of this world also fall.

When we place our joy only upon Him, we will never, no matter what, lose. We may and will encounter times of strife and sorrow and even tragedy but our joy and peace is held in His hands not what we have lost. These are exercises in obedience brought upon in a fallen world that will someday be restored to its original intent.

Until that day, we must extend our focus and our vision beyond the boundaries that seek to contain us. This requires a discipline in obedience that sometimes will seem to use the same exertion as the physical equivalent of climbing the highest mountain, swimming the farthest sea or running the longest race.

It is not easy to escape the bondage that this world would intend for us to live our lives. We aren't the first ones to encounter this. Even Paul had to find contentment outside of this world and he did it with such discipline that he found contentment regardless of his worldly circumstances.

This doesn't mean that the pain doesn't occur or that the tears don't fall but it comes by squaring ones shoulders and walking on. Focusing not on the pain of this world but rather on the joy of salvation that will be for eternity.

Where does your true center lie today?

Where is your joy found?

What specific action plan can you take today to live worthy?

Lifting Up Holy Hands | 1 Timothy 2:8

Therefore I want the men everywhere to pray, lifting up holy hands without anger or disputing.

Holy is most often reserved for describing our Heavenly Father, the sanctities in the church, even water. But how often do we look at our own hands and see them as God sees them? Holy.

Is it because we tend to spend more time using our hands for the things of this world instead of for things Holy? Can we really lift up the same hands to our Father that we use to angrily motion to the car that just cut in front of us? Can we use the same hands offered to Him that we use to hit those we love, take that next drink, blur the lines of our lives or use for lingering forbidden touches, whether real or virtual?

Do we keep ourselves Holy?

There's a fine line, yes? And what this world will call Holy, God will probably dismiss so how can we be asked to do the seemingly undoable?

Perhaps, we need to change drastically. Perhaps, we need to seek more time in prayer than we do arguing about how to pray and whom should pray, maybe we should just pray.

There's a seeking world out there looking for something, looking for Truth. It's a fearful reality that when they look in our churches, instead of Holy Hands, they find legalism, cliques and superficial perfection.

Live Worthy

They find competition and marks at which they are measured against and they walk away disenchanted with God when truthfully they hadn't encounters God at all and instead quite possibly the opposite.

These are choices we choose every day. We, alone, can decide to lay down our pride, to lay down what we deserve and follow Him. He is the reward. Nothing else.

Is that enough?

There is no guaranteed raise coming at the end of this. There's eternal life but in this world, we are not guaranteed reward based on performance. There's no happy-ever after clause that says if you put in 5, 10, 20 years of hard servitude you will be able to retire comfortably. Look at Paul. Look at Christ. So, what do we position ourselves for? It is all a facade. Smoke screens and mirages.

Instead, we seek Holiness. We choose not be angry. How? Pray hard. But it's bigger than us. Then pray harder. This is not about the disputes at hand but rather a bigger battle with implications that we simply can't fathom.

Choose to live worthy.

If the action that we performed with our hands were written on them, what words would appear?

What is our motive for Holiness?

What specific action plan can you take today to live worthy?

I Want The Women | 1 Timothy 2: 9-10

I also want the women to dress modestly, with decency and propriety, adorning themselves, not with elaborate hairstyles or gold or pearls or expensive clothes, but with good deeds, appropriate for women who profess to worship God.

I want the women.

And with this statement, the world has attempted time and time again to take control of how a woman should be. This has resulted many of our sisters being controlled and oppressed by the misguided thoughts of men. Women who are afraid to be who God has created them to be. Women who follow an earthly man and not their Heavenly Father along with the lies and mirages that satan weaves.

Submission was intended to coexist with a husband whose own heart was aligned with Christ's desires. A husband who seeks God's will for his life and his family. A husband who walks humbly, Christ-like and exhibits the fruits of the spirit in his own life. He is described to demonstrate love, joy, peace, patience, kindness, goodness, faithfulness, gentleness and self-control to those who he serves, both outside and inside his own home. This man will humbly place God's desires ahead of his own thoughts and will lift his family up with grace and mercy.

Many times, though, the darkness of this world taints this picture darkening a union intended to be used for God's favor. Instead of fruits of the Spirit, we find pride and the need to control.

We find men that should walk humbly stomp with their "God-given" authority lording it over the very one they should treasure most. Unknowingly, they fall prey to satan's attack and they become authorities on the proper behavior of women while the women around them suffer, greatly.

They begin to have downcast eyes. Their hearts begin harden and their soul cries out to our Father. They want to serve Him. They desire to obey and be submissive as He has called them to be but something doesn't seem right.

They become caught up in a world of legalism focusing on dos and don'ts and completely missing the Truth. Some are bound and greatly oppressed while many of us continually struggle with whom we, as a Christian women, should be. Confused about what we are "allowed" to do always judged by those who have fixated on how we should be.

And how should we be? We should be Christ-like. We should seek Him above all else with great discernment. We must be wise with humility and filled with compassion for those who seek to control in order to fulfill their own earthly needs. We must pray, read His word faithfully and trust Him. We must know Him, above all else, we must follow Him.

Submissiveness by Godly design is freeing. Submissiveness under the world's definition is quite the opposite.

Who are you in the reality of the world?

How do you demonstrate the privilege God has bestowed upon you?

What specific action plan can you take today to live worthy?

Quietly and submissively | 1 Timothy 2:11

A woman should learn in quietness and full submission.

Paul wrote this in regards to how women and men should relate with one another in a church service quite possibly in a specific church service during his contemporary time.

And yet, these nine words have created quite a tapestry on which satan has weaved some of the greatest of lies. Lies that either causes women to be less than what God created them to be or lies that cause women to overcompensate for what God created them to be. Lies that draw us out of the true intentions of His creation.

While there are a host of arguments and commentaries that will attempt to shed light on Paul's direction, there is still an unsettlement within this world. An unsettlement that creates distraction from the Truth. An unsettlement, that if we allow it, will focus on the issue of women instead of Him. I, myself, can take such question of this statement that I miss my Father's intentions and become ensnarled in the world's deceit.

We can only imagine what church services were like in Paul's time. Evidently, he had a group of women that were extremely disruptive and disrespectful within the church services. Fueled by false teachers and doctrine, they distracted from the teachings of God's Word with public outcry and emotional teaching without sound doctrine. They were called down, so to speak, so that they and others might hear the Truth.

What would Paul's words be today to the women sitting in our churches? Most services are quiet and respectful with very minimal public outcries. Services in which everyone tries to blend in, sit through the sermon and leave. Well- behaved for all appearances.

But how often are we truly fully submissive during the teachings of God's Word so that our spirit is quiet and we soak up His message?

Do we listen with reverence? Do we focus all of our attention on what God is trying impart?

Or dare do I say, that we fall prey to satan's snares quite possibly, just more subtly? We find ourselves for the first time all week sitting in a quiet place. Our weary and tired bodies and souls fall to soak in, not His Word, but rather peace and quiet. Or maybe, we are already focusing on the week ahead of us by planning the grocery list, children's schedule and the other activities of the week?

Or we watch others and we silently compare our family with theirs and our lives with their own. Do we measure up? Have we surrounded ourselves with the right friends and then we notice that someone else is talking to someone else and we have been left out? Or we silently suffer just trying to be.

Would not Paul's words ring just as true today?

We must learn in quietness and be fully submissive. We must learn to quiet our very souls so that we can hear God's word. So that we can hear His voice. Why even attend if not to listen? We must sit in obedient submissiveness to our Father so that we are strengthened and encouraged.

As we learn to walk in quiet submissiveness to Him, we will start to find contentment in who we are. The arguments and debates of this world will fall away and His Truth will stand-alone. We will no longer fall prey to the chaos and noise of this world that only seeks to confuse and disillusion us and to steal of joy, our hope.

This isn't an argument about who lords over whom but rather a directive to submit to the One who created us all so that we might be found worthy of the call.

Quietly and submissively.

Where does your mind travel when you sit in the sanctuary of the church?

What emotions does the word submission evoke within your soul?

What specific action plan can you take today to live worthy?

Silent Obedience | 1 Timothy 2:12

I do not permit a woman to teach or have authority over a man; she must be silent.

Paul used a Greek word here that when translated into English means to have an attitude of quietness and composure as opposed to an alternative Greek word that would call for complete silence. He was speaking specifically to the Ephesian church, which was filled with new women believers who were seemingly becoming more and more into themselves proclaiming loudly instead of learning and maturing.

As women, I think we tend to walk a fine line in this world. Being a "strong" woman, myself, this seems to be an area that satan will use to create chaos and noise. As a woman begins to walk in obedience, finding both her strength and favor in the Lord, satan observing that favor will dwell up criticism to try to avert her path and discourage her within.

Yet, God created her to be strong.

Within in her lies the strength to move mountains, part the seas and heal the sick. Created with the ability to lead and lead greatly, satan will attempt to discredit her ability, many times using God's word against her. Often times, he uses people within the church to try to hit her where it would hurt most.

And without God's grace and careful discernment, she may begin to falter. Instead of seeking His Word and direction, she may begin to turn to others for advice or an image on which to mirror herself against. Given enough opposition, she may turn completely from Him and join the world, which will embrace her innate strength and will marvel at her ability. Yet, as she dives further into the world, she will turn farther and farther away from His plan for her life.

So, then how as strong women should we be?

I have learned that God created me to be strong for a reason.

And He makes no mistakes.

However, as with any gift from the Father, we must discipline ourselves and use it with the reverence in which it was intended. We were created to use our strength for His Glory. We were created to use our strength for the purpose in which He created it to be used. Period.

This isn't a battle against the "sexes". This isn't a battle to determine equal rights. This is not even a battle upon equality.

This is bigger than that.

This is a battle for souls. A battle that is fought not only on the field that we walk upon but also in the spiritual realm. This is a battle that has eternal repercussions. So does it really matter if I, as a women can or can't do certain things based on man's interpretation to God's Word? When I set aside my pride and ego, when I set aside my fleshy desires to be equal; no, it matters not at all. What truly matters is am I using what God has given me for the purpose that He intended it to be used?

I can fight all day the battle to preach from a pulpit that has been delegated as being only for men. And, given today's political arena, may quite possibly win. But what would I really accomplish? Worldly recognition at the cost of dissension and division of God's people as a result of my own disobedience.

I serve Him. Christ and Christ alone. Out of that flows goodness that this world will never understand. As women, we have to allow ourselves to let go of the things of this world and focus on being Godly women. He will guide us every step of the way.

Where do you resist obedience and submission?

Where has God called you to be strong?

What specific action plan can you take today to live worthy?

Holy Balance | 1 Timothy 2:13-14

For Adam was formed first, then Eve. And Adam was not the one deceived; it was the women who was deceived and became a sinner.

There is an order to God's world and a method to the madness. A balance.

And, yet we live in a world that follows extremes and highlights the chaos instead of recognizing the balance that falls into place when the foundation is Truth.

This doesn't mean that the storms will be calmed and that troubles will cease to exist but rather that the soul within has a peace that depends not upon the happenings in this world. Our lives can literally be torn apart, our very homes destroyed and financial ruin within site but the balance is determined by a Peace that cannot be shaken no matter what.

So as we believe in God, we must look within and honestly inquire upon ourselves whether or not we believe Him. Silly question perhaps, however, if we put as much emphasis in our believing Him as we do in our belief in Him, this world would have nothing on us.

Nothing.

We would find ourselves secure regardless of our day. Sound sleep regardless of our night. Standing firm regardless of our task. Because He is Who He is, isn't He?

Instead we, as believers in Him, find ourselves many times miserable. Commiserating with our brothers and sisters in Christ at our lot in life and at our lot in this world. We find ourselves even commiserating with those of this world at our lot in life and at our lot in this world quickly forgetting the privilege that we have been given. Privilege to serve Him. Him, the Almighty. In light of that, does it really matter? Does it matter at all?

I have found that to glorify Him is to glorify Him at all times. Even if it is with my best of friends, small group or gathering of friends, I stand representing Him regardless at what comes my way. Him. When I constantly complain time after time, when I wallow in self-pity, when I indulge in the unfairness of me, I in no way glorify Him. Not at all. I am called to be Christ-like and Christ has never once wallowed in His love for me. Not one time.

But it's good for us, isn't it? We shouldn't hold it in. Perhaps, but perhaps the One whom we should be commiserating with is the One who can make the changes in ourselves. As the father of the possessed boy said to Jesus, "Help me with my unbelief." He converses straight to the King, "Help me."

Coursing within us is the power to move mountains, calm the storms and love the unlovable. With all of that potential within, how can we possibly fail?

Yet, so often we do. We listen to the whispers satan weaves and we compound it by confiding in others, weakening in their own personal stance, and we begin to slump instead of stand. We begin to wonder what the purpose really is. We begin to seek all measures to try to fix the slippery slope of despair.

The deception continues.

There is only one permanent fix. Only one. Father, help us with our unbelief. Help us step on continually in faith and faith alone knowing that Your foundation is secure. Let no words pass our lips that do not glorify you. No words.

Where do you turn when hardship comes your way?

What thoughts come to mind when your world seems to fall apart?

What specific action plan can you take today to live worthy?

Casualties of Spin | 1 Timothy 2:15

But women will be saved through childbearing-if they continue in faith, love and holiness with propriety.

Propriety, the state or quality of conforming to conventionally accepted standards of behavior or morals, the standards being faith, love and holiness. One woman, through the pain and labors of childbirth, gave birth to a Son who would bring salvation to us all and our part is to live lives of faith, love and holiness.

It is simple, really.

We either do or we don't. We either choose to be obedient or we don't.

We can spend our whole lives trying to argue points of contention. We can even find ourselves elevating our own agendas while we twist and turn words, mix and matching Scriptures while spinning Truth.

But Truth does not spin. It is what it is.

We can walk through the halls of our churches and take offense to those who don't speak to us. We can find fault in the pastor's words and the choir's songs as we scope out the "entertainment" of the morning. Complaining time and time again of the lack of depth to our spiritual walk, we place blame on anyone near and far. We claim we are searching with all our hearts, yet, we never find.

But maybe we do.

Perhaps we find Truth and realize the contrast that our lives reflect. Perhaps we simply just don't want to change.

Holiness, love and faith but only if it is on our terms.

Only if, the cost is equal to all parties involved and, only if, we are well rewarded.

We've become a society conditioned to be rewarded for jobs well done.

We eat healthy for a week and we reward ourselves with a treat. We win and we get a medal. We forget that our very first reward was bestowed before we had ever breathed our first breath. We were rewarded undeserved. We were rewarded because He loved us first. We may do everything right and quite possibly will find ourselves judged harshly by this world ridiculed not revered.

As the sun sets and rises each day, we each come closer and closer to the moment when we will meet Him face to face. At that moment, it will not matter who called us what, who recognized us, who talked to us or who even loved us. What will matter will be our response, our personal journal, and our own choice to be.

When Tae died, I wondered at how I would ever find joy in this world again. I wondered how I would ever laugh and how I would ever care. Quickly, Jesus responded that I would find joy, happiness and compassion through Him and Him alone.

As we discipline ourselves to focus on Him, our eyes will be opened to what really matters and what does not.

Faith, Love.

Holy.

And this is how we should be.

Where does your joy come from, honestly? Is it all from Him?

What part of His Truth do you choose not to accept as Truth?

What specific action plan can you take today to live worthy?

Noble Task | 1 Timothy 3:1

Here is a trustworthy saying: whoever aspires to be an overseer desires a noble task.

More than a title. More than a position of authority or control. A noble task.

A task of such noble charge that satan will stop at nothing to attempt to taint the Holiness. A noble task that extends beyond the clutches of this world. A task whose foundation is eternal.

Yet, we struggle against the principalities of this world. A world that will tell us that we must be recognized, that we must be in control and yield to none. That our direction and ours alone is the one we will follow. All the while proclaiming to be followers of Him while seeking recognition of others.

We will work tirelessly throughout the day and night to create just the perfect work. A banquet, a conference, a church service, a retreat, a lesson and the list goes on and on. Perhaps it is not recognition at all that we seek but rather our unrelenting tasking comes from within. A balance that we continually struggle to obtain. We work and work to create just the right plan. Our motives are seemingly pure yet before we know the task takes on earthly forms instead of nobility.

And we fail.

And in this place is where we find the true nobility of our cause. When we step aside or fall. He steps in our stead and He carries His cause. A noble task. He brings our focus back to Him. He restores our joy and fulfills our soul.

Whether our task becomes worldly because of our blatant disobedience or as a result of our quest for perfection, the result is the same. Satan has achieved our distraction from the King. He has stolen joy and in its place we find despair, frustration and we begin to believe that nothing is good enough.

Instead of reveling in serving those He has given us, we begin to resent and avoid.

A noble task.

A task that calls for humility and discipline to execute. A task that says, "Your will and not mine." A task that really is okay when it is not our will. In our minds, we can create a pseudo-reality in which we envision the future and what it will be when in reality, we can do nothing of the sort. And when reality falls short of what our mind had built up, whether that be marriage, a job, a relationship we lose joy in what we actually experience.

Live for today. Focus on today's noble tasks at hand. Prepare for tomorrow with humility for a tomorrow that may never be but this moment is real and for a purpose. Don't wait planning to do God's work at the next event or mission trip. Our moment is now. Pity the soul who stands before the King filled with regret because his time came before the "event".

The event is now.

Why do you, truthfully, do what you do for the church?

What thoughts come to mind while you are serving?

What specific action plan can you take today to live worthy?

Realities of this World | 1 Timothy 3:2-3

Now the overseer is to be above reproach, faithful to his wife, temperate, self-controlled, respectable, hospitable, able to teach, not given to drunkenness, not violent but gentle, not quarrelsome, not a lover of money.

And the world will call us weak, crazy and disturbed. We will be taunted, ridiculed and provoked. The world will simply not understand.

And that is okay.

This world is not our home, is neither our refuge nor our Judge. We must use great discernment as we daily traverse this earth. We are told to store up our treasures in heaven and to focus on things eternal.

There is a fine dance between walking in obedience and walking in the flesh. We must balance ourselves upon His solid foundation. Truth. Cautioned against being quarrelsome and entering into battle that has no eternal value, we must be steadfast in our walk.

Yet, our emotions are real and we will struggle daily against the desires of our flesh to be right, to be loved, to be accepted and to have peace. We will even struggle to be and to have something that will not ever be true but rather a superficial mist that dissipates when Light shines upon it.

A mist that seeks to keep our eyes closed to the realities of this world. A mist that will smooth the rough edges and will disguise the free fall below. A mist that simply ensnarls and entangles us with the sole purpose to discredit and detain. As we engage in worldly superficial battles, we take ourselves out of the eternal battle for souls.

So we walk humbly and love greatly, even the unlovable, sometimes perhaps from afar. We leave loved ones and loved places to follow in obedience. We above all else seek Truth and Truth alone.

Where is your view of this world clouded with the mist of darkness?

What has He called you to do that goes against the realities of this world?

What specific action plan can you take today to live worthy?

Auto-pilot | 1 Timothy 3:4

He must manage his own family well and see that his children obey him with proper respect.

Manage. Actively engaged. Purposeful creation.

Good families don't just happen. They require purposeful intention focused on that specific family's desires. They require the greatest humility and unconditional love. They require a foundation that is saturated in grace and mercy.

So much of our world today is lived on autopilot. We wake up, work, go to bed and repeat. We live for those few moments in time when we can escape our reality. Eagerly anticipating that next holiday, vacation or retreat just so we can survive to go on to the next moment of escape to reconnect with our families, with our kids and with our husbands and wives.

We live to escape our own lives!

And our children watch day after day.

They observe too often values that are misplaced, integrity that is simply debatable and joy relative. They watch as marriages fail, violence abounds and God's Word is a book we carry to church. They quickly learn what is important to us and what makes us excited. A 4.0 GPA, the winning goal, the top prize and the coolest friends gain them recognition from not only the world but also ourselves. We plot and plan every aspect of their day to create in them the most amazing opportunities.

Yet, we have fallen sorrowfully short to the most important opportunity of all. Quite frankly, the only opportunity that we should invest our time, talents and focus.

Christ.

We hand our children over to programs designed to engage them. We take them to church and drop them off at their respective doors and when it is all completed, we walk away. And we wonder, what is the world coming to?

The battle for souls begins early. The battle for souls begins intentionally. Unfortunately, we don't engage until the enemy has drawn the first blood. We have got to be intentional. We have got to live purposefully. They will model us. They will. But if they don't find anything to connect to or to model, they will look elsewhere and the enemy of this world will welcome them with open arms.

This is something we can stop. We can set aside our drive to conquer this world and commit to be driven to protect our own families. This doesn't mean to embrace legalism and demand respect but rather to walk with love and humility and to teach as Jesus taught. The children flocked to Him.

Do ours flock to us?

They do for a time. Until too many times they are brushed away as we talk on our phones, watch TV, down another drink; take another pill or anything to help us feel in control of a world that we will never conquer.

Either death or Christ is coming. One of the other should be our focus. The time in between is the opportunity to live lives in preparation for that day.

Are you preparing?

If your children were asked what is the most important lesson that you want them to learn, how would they respond?

Outline your last week, how often did your children, or those around you, see you in worship, prayer and other time focused on God?

What specific action plan can you take today to live worthy?

All Or Nothing | 1 Timothy 3:5

If anyone does not know how to manage his own family, how can he take care of God's church?

I used to be a "leave it all on the field" type of person. Modeled after a player on a team who consistently strives to give 110%, that was my drive.

Until God revealed to me that we weren't meant to "play" life that way. We weren't meant to "leave it all out on the field" with nothing to bring home. Whether it be the mission field, the church, our jobs or school, they are not meant to be our sole focus with our families consistently getting the leftovers which amounts to a dry negative number if we are giving 110% to the outside.

We push ourselves harder and harder to meet deadlines while balancing families and charitable events. We strive to create harmony, yet, continually fall short when the hours of commitment greatly outweigh the hours in the day.
We hurriedly rush through our lives trying to create more time in which to accomplish what we seemingly have to accomplish.

Yet, the walls continually close in, deadlines become shorter, our children become less pliable and our marriages begin to demand more. A demand that we know is legitimate, yet, we will argue vehemently that we are already giving it all.

And, we are.

We are giving all of ourselves to be strewn across our day. We are so busy and so scheduled that when we find ourselves at pivotal moments we have nothing more to give.

We become resentful to those in our lives who begin to demand more. We pull inward as we steady ourselves to continue down a path that is insurmountable. A path that we have created with the help of the enemy in this world. A path that says that we can do it all.

But we were never meant to do it all.

We were created for a purpose. Just because we can do something doesn't mean that we were meant to do it. As humility begins to edge out the pride in our lives, we will find peace in who we really are. We will find peace in who He created us to be. When we begin to find that place, our lives will begin to change. We will start to find peace within instead of continual chaos. Our souls will be quieted and fed instead of continually starved and neglected. We will find freedom.

We will find that we have all that we need to do what He has purposed us to do. What we seemed to have lacked in time, energy and resources now seems to have no limit because we are walking the path we were created to walk as opposed to walking a path the world has tried to thrust upon us. No task is insurmountable when the task has been assigned by the One who will complete it through us.

Commit to walk slower today. Listen within and follow.

Where in your life are you neglecting in order to continue performing to other's standards?

Where in the reality of importance does God appear in your life?

What specific action plan can you take today to live worthy?

Weave Of Lies | 1 Timothy 3:6

He must not be a recent convert, or he may become conceited and fall under the same judgment as the devil.

Satan.

Our adversary. Our enemy who seeks to destroy and what it can't destroy, seeks to tarnish and fade. He seeks to steal our joy, our blessings and our focus.

And too many times, he is successful. Too many times.

It seems as if he can take the experiences of our life and wring out of them every drop of anger, despair and betrayal. He can conjure up memories, either real or fantasy, from years prior that oftentimes can bring us right back to that time and place and emotions. He seeks to distract us from our true purpose and our true focus because while we are allured back into the past, we are not purposeful in the future. We aren't even present in the present.

He attempts to define us by what is has happened to us not by Whose we are. Before we know it, we have spent months or years in that same place, tormented by the same thoughts of the past never finding reconciliation or restoration but rather the same wound that bleeds the same bright red blood when the scab is scraped off. Before we know it, we have missed opportunity upon opportunity to be with those God has given is to love not just to be present in the room but also to really experience the joys and blessings of this world.

Before we know it, our hearts have hardened and we have become so familiar with the thoughts within that it is inconceivable that there could be any other way.

This is the life we have been dealt. The game that we have been played.

As his lies weave on and on.

A month or so after Taellor died, we realized that we were at another turning point. Images and emotions kept trying to push into our minds and our hearts. Images and emotions that if we chose to entertain would have left us paralyzed and broken. Images and emotions that only the one who would seek to destroy us would bring into our lives.

As we sat across from each other one evening, we decided that her death would not define us. Death would not steal anymore from us. Satan would not steal anymore from us. No more. He can wring, twist and tear all he wishes but we choose to glorify Him. We choose to live worthy.

And with that came freedom. Freedom not to entertain or dwell in the darkness but to entertain only the Truth and Light. It doesn't mean that we love her less, but rather that we celebrate where she is and we continue the journey here living worthy as opposed to merely surviving.

What we have found is that this is true in all things not just the big things. Whether I have been cut-off in traffic or have had my feelings hurt, I can choose to either let satan use it to hurt me further or I can stop it.

Satan doesn't win. He doesn't. Sometimes we forget the power that dwells within us. Power that we just have to choose to engage. We choose our response. We are no one's victim. They may hurt, betray, lie and steal from us but that doesn't change who we are. We are children of the King and we will live humbly as such.

What in your past does satan continually try to cast upon your present day?

What thoughts come to mind when you try to break away from the past?

What specific action plan can you take today to live worthy?

Simply a Trap | 1 Timothy 3:7

He must also have a good reputation with outsiders, so that he will not fall into disgrace and into the devil's trap.

It's a trap.

A masquerade, a slight of heart, a play on words, a glance here and movement there.

We see it so well in other people's lives. We see their trappings, their shortcoming and the devil's work in their lives. We see the husband or wife that works too much. We observe an obsession taking root. We see pride slipping into a humble life. We observe as the facade is slowly built and then slowly starts to unravel. We watch and we wait, too often, out of touch and at a distance. Close enough to see yet with enough distance to be uninvolved.

In fact, we dare not to bring him to mind until something bad happens. Quite possibly out of fear that we might summons him to remember us. So we walk ill prepared and seemingly unaware as the traps are sat around us.

The words. The whispers. The walls begin to close in.

And, we remember. We seek His armor and we prepare after the trap had been laid. We seek armor often after the door has been tripped. Then we realize, into the very core of who we are that we are trapped and we seek our God with everything we are.

But, what if the door to the trap never actually falls and we never realize the walls of the trap that surrounds us? What if the trap itself is the very life that we seek to portray as perfect? What if our very busy life has become so big of a trap itself, that the devil doesn't even have to trip the wire? For we have fallen so far in, that we don't even recognize the distance that has been woven between us and our Creator.

But it's all good, yes? The work, the family, the home, the serving and the list goes on and on. We forget that none of it matters not one bit of it matters if our hearts are waiting for the praise of man or the recognition of our work.

So, we seek on filling our world with stuff. Stuff that will be here for today and quite possibly gone tomorrow. We seek a reputation that is recognized in this world. Our plan. Our name. Our contribution.

Ours. The devil knows pride all too well for it was his own downfall. Even within our churches, the trappings of pride runs rampant with conceit not too far behind. Unfortunately the door to the trapping of pride rarely falls; instead it stays open as we walk deeper and deeper becoming more conceited and less like Him.

What will it take for us to realize that none of this is about us? None of it. Yet, all of this is about us. In this world, we should find Our Creator, not try to be the creator. In this world, we should honor Him not ourselves. In this world, we should serve others not out of duty or pride but out of a joyful heart for the more we step outside of the self the world would have us portray, we experience more and more of Him. The more we realize what is real and what is smoke the more that it will fade.

We will seek not for our name to be known but for His. Really. We won't just portray this to the world but we will feel it deep in the core of who we are. It doesn't matter who receives credit or who experiences the blessing of distribution. What will matter will be our obedience in doing our part and that is where we will find joy. Satan doesn't know that place. The place where we lay it all down at the cross and say, "His will, not mine."

It's a journey where we will stumble and fall but it is also a choice and a battle we will constantly fight within ourselves. We can't have it both ways. Either we seek the praise of man or the praise of Him. Our choice. What I do know though is that when this life is over, the praise of man stays here in this world.

Live lives aware of traps constantly being set. Don't live in fear of them but rather in the steadfast armor from our Father.

Live worthy.

Where do you find your identity?

Who are you in this world?

What specific action plan can you take today to live worthy?

Worthy Of Respect | 1 Timothy 3:8

Deacons, likewise, are to be men worthy of respect, sincere, not indulging in much wine, and not pursuing dishonest gain.

Not entitled to respect, not to be respected but worthy of respect. As a world focused on authority and control, there is an implied respect that is expected which either comes by the position or title of a person. Students should show respect to their teachers. Employees show respect to their employers. Constituents give respect to their elected officials and so on. There are people in all of our lives that demonstrate respect for each of us simply because of the position that we hold.

But what happens when all titles and man-given positions are stripped away? Would we be found worthy of respect based on the merit of our character alone?

There's the saying that 'the end justifies the means.'. A healthy bottom line, great bedside manner, good when it counts. But when doesn't it count? What is healthy about a manner of life that may end in a robust plump account but leaves casualties in its wake? When did good manners only count at someone's bedside?

We live our lives as if only specific bursts of life count.

We live our lives doing good deeds and work when it is scheduled on our calendar. We look forward to a week here and there, in which we will serve Him with all our hearts such as a Saturday set apart to do service work. But what about the other weeks in the year? What about the people that surround us every single day?

What about the people that we live life with? Do they find us worthy of respect?

We've bought into the lies that in order to succeed, in order to come out on top that sometimes the lines get blurry. Sometimes, the sacrifice becomes deeper than our time and talents.

Eroding away at our character and integrity, we begin to live different lives depending on where we are and whom we are with.

Is it possible that the ever-elusive " top", success or next step is just a facade? A facade distracting us from what really is the main purpose and the true accomplishment. Our true purpose here will be found only in Him and His measure of success looks completely different from this world's. This is where we will find joy. This is where we will find an inner peace that will be indescribable no matter where we are. Some of us will hold high and lofty positions while some of us will walk among trash dumps, yet, we will each be fulfilling the true purpose of our lives.

Our true purpose being found in living obedient to Him however that might look, living worthy every moment of every day and seeing the bigger picture of this world instead of the carrots that satan dangles in front of us. It is about the small things, the gentle touches and joy the penetrates the darkness. It is about being okay with walking with, yet, apart. It is about seeking His will above our own and not praising ourselves for being a martyr in the situation.

Live Worthy

And through all of this true respect will come, even from those who would seek to destroy us. A respect that is not understood in the world yet that is recognized as being magnificent. A respect that withstands the fire be it a corrupt system, a late deadline or a busy family.

A respect that is real.

Live worthy.

What are the circumstances that you allow your integrity to be blurred?

If others were observing your day-to-day life, would they see you the same no matter whether you are at home, work, church and play?

What specific action plan can you take today to live worthy?

Deep Roots | 1 Timothy 3:9

They must keep hold of the deep truths of the faith with a clear conscious.

Deep truths of the faith.

Faith. A seemingly mystery to man, yet revealed to us by our Creator. The same faith as Abraham, Noah, David and Rahab. The same faith that parted the seas and saw burning bushes. The same faith that still moves mountains even today.

That faith.

Yet somewhere along the way, our faith has become more superficial. Our faith has become not a faith of legends but instead a faith of mostly history. A faith that seems to have forgotten that we serve a living God who moves just as greatly today as He did in days past.

Just as great. We speak of this but do we live as this?

At what point within our Christian faith, did it become a sacrifice to serve Him? When did it become acceptable to use the word to describe our journey walking with Him a sacrifice? When did we insert the word sacrifice for privilege?

We walk on this earth by His grace. Creation was created for His glory. This is all about Him every moment, every day. It should be a given that we would serve, a given that we would love, a given that we would be and a given that we will walk worthy. Not a sacrifice but a privilege to honor our King.

A sacrifice was what happened at the Cross. A sacrifice was what God asked for when He told Abraham to take Isaac. A sacrifice. Yet, we have begun to think that it is a sacrifice to teach a Sunday School class, a sacrifice to serve the poor, a sacrifice to study His Word, a sacrifice to and each of us can fill in our own blank. It has become a sacrifice to do anything that we choose not to do.

Every day that we choose to honor Him, everyday that we choose to live our lives focused on Him is not a sacrifice but rather simply living as we were created to live. We were created for this. The other "stuff" that we allow to fill our lives and clutter our hearts and minds is merely a distraction from our true purpose. The world has become such a distraction, that we have decided that when we must deviate from our worldly lives we are sacrificing.

But maybe we are simply being obedient to Him. The devil will try to make it more than it is. He will try to take our pride and ego and try to make pseudo- martyrs because that's what he does. He seeks to destroy.

May we live worthy.

Where, in your life, do you feel that you are sacrificing your time for the Kingdom?

Where can you experience the privilege of serving Him more?

What specific action plan can you take today to live worthy?

Tested | 1 Timothy 3:10

They must first be tested; and then if there is nothing against them, let them serve as deacons.

We live in a world that strives first, it seems, to be politically correct and to not offend. Everyone wins. All who participate are tried to be equally recognized regardless of true ability or growth. So as to keep the peace or not to hurt feelings, everyone wins.

But everyone doesn't win. They don't.

We all don't have the same strengths and abilities. We don't. We are all created differently with different abilities and characteristics. We are. Different walks, different paths and different choices have molded each of us differently and, sometimes, no matter how badly a position or title might be sought it is not ours to have.

And that is okay.

Just as we seem to grow and mature most when we are in the valleys of our faith, so is our character and true faith shown to the world. It is easy to call oneself worthy but a completely different story to live as one is worthy every day.

They must first be tested.

Who are we really when a storm comes our way? Do we respond as we have previously taught one should? Do we rest in Him as we advise others to when we find ourselves surrounded in darkness? Do we seek His Word for guidance even when it guides against the grain of this world?

Live Worthy

It wasn't easy to praise Him during this time of our daughter leaving this world. I look back during that time and what I see in our response was sheer obedience. An obedience steeped greatly in our desire to live worthy and to simply praise Him.

It might have appeared easy but some days it was a minute by minute conscious choice to forego the guidance of this world and look straight on into Him. For us, there was no other choice.

Yes, I know that there was another choice. A choice to grieve, as the world would have us grieve. A choice to take a break from our "faith" and be "real", but where else do you go when your faith is all you have? Where else do you go when your faith is the only string left on a rapidly fraying rope?

There was no other choice.

When we select leaders, teachers, friends and when we look at our own lives, we must be comfortable with looking into the valleys as well as the mountaintop accomplishments. For within the valley, we will find true faith. A faith that withstands. A faith that is unshakable and real. A faith that I would enter any battle with. A faith that is firm. Anyone can sing praises on the mountaintop but only a few will sing praises in the valley.

A faith that has been tested and is true.

How do you respond when storms come your way?

If others were observing your walking in the storm, would they see joy from the Lord or a reflection of the world?

What specific action plan can you take today to live worthy?

Temperate | 1 Timothy 3:11

In the same way, their wives are to be women worthy of respect, not malicious talkers but temperate and trustworthy in everything.

Showing moderation and self- restraint in everything.

Not only in public. Not only in private matters. Not only within the family nor outside the family. But with all things.

Moderation. Self-restraint.

Yet, we live in a world that thrives on excessiveness. Whether we splurge here or there or we indulge in between, do we live lives of self-restraint? Do we live lives of moderation? Of course, the first question to ask would be against what measure? I dare to respond that if one has the luxury to ask such a question than quite possibly we wouldn't even recognize lives of temperate or lives of moderation.

If you earned more than $1500 last year, you are considered to be in the top 20% of income earners in the world. Does our lives feel like we are? If you have sufficient food, clothes, transportation and housing, you are considered in the top 15% of the world's wealthy? Do we live as if we are in the top 15%? If you earned over $50,000 last year, you are in the top 1% in the world. Top 1%.

Wow.

And, yet, we live lives striving for the next big thing, the next promotion, the next meal, the next house, car, clothing, shoes, and toys.

We live wanting more and more but never feeling quite satisfied that we've gotten enough. We live lives measured and gratified by material gains. We live lives not ever feeling wealthy enough.

Even though, we sit among the top wealthiest in the world.

We are called to live lives of moderation. We are called to live lives of self- restraint. Many of us have been greatly, greatly blessed and yet we don't recognize our own lot in this world. Instead, we see our lot compared to the "Jones" next door and our lot seems oh so small. The reality is though that we serve a big God who rules over a big world and our lot in this big world is enormous.

Enormous.

We have been blessed for a reason. We have been given the gift of education and literacy, stability and health, security and wealth. We have been given the privilege to make a difference for His kingdom. Do we embrace that privilege? Or do we squander our blessings on our own lives waiting until we have "extra" to help others? Do we strive to meet our own desires, dreams and wants before helping another reach their basic needs?

We will be called to give an account of the gifts we have been given. Do we use them worthy? Do we live lives of self-restraint and moderation?

Do we live worthy?

Do you give regularly to the Kingdom of your time, talent and treasures?

Do you give out of what we have or only out of the excess?

What specific action plan can you take today to live worthy?

Pointed Towards Christ | 1 Timothy 3:12

A deacon must be the husband of but one wife and must manage his children and his household well.

We can choose to build our homes up or we can tear them down. It's our choice.

We all long for a household of happiness, love and respect but what do we do to cultivate the atmosphere we desire, the acceptance that we yearn, the place where we can be at rest?

We seek a husband that revels in us, protects and loves. We dream of children that will grow to be close to our hearts and friends that will speak love in our lives. Do we cultivate as such in our own life?

If the complete feel of our home reflected our own hearts, what would the mirror show?

Are we consistent, forgiving, merciful and gracious? Are we firm and sincere, truthful and calm? Do we manage our homes in a Christ-like manner? Are we hospitable?

Do we manage our homes as we would manage our Sunday school class or church service or even a missions project? So many reflect that they aren't the same back home as they are in the field. They reflect that they can love more freely here and give grace and mercy and that they choose to see joy.

Yet in our own homes, we see everything that isn't good enough, everything that needs to be changed and everything wrong.

We spend our marriages finding fault and our children's lives finding places that need improvement and through it all, day after day, we lose the opportunity to see the joy that was there all along.

Not the joy that the world treasures. A superficial plastic sort of joy but rather joy that withstands time. Joy that transcends tragedy.

Joy that is eternal. Joy that surrounds us every day if we only would have sought it in our present instead of at the end of the day, year or life when we reflect that we will do better next time. We will find joy next time.

But we can't, for that time, that opportunity to see joy is gone forever.

Choose to manage our families purposefully focused on joy focused on Christ and we will find Him there, always.

Do you strive to be hospitable to your family that live day to day in your home?

How do you make each day a purposeful day?

What specific action plan can you take today to live worthy?

Serve Well | 1 Timothy 3:13

Those who have served well gain an excellent standing and great assurance in their faith in Christ Jesus.

And how shall we serve? We shall serve well.

There is something empowering about serving others. Something invigorating to our very souls to forego our own desires, walk in humility and put someone else's needs before our own. For no pay, recognition or self-elevation, but solely for the privilege to serve a child of the King.

In our world today, this goes against the common school of thought. Of course, one should do charitable work and one should give to charitable organizations but that's where the difference begins. This has nothing to do with obligations or charity and all to about being His hands. His feet.

Satan will try to discourage and confuse by offering arguments, excuses and reasons why we should serve other in order to gain notoriety or excuses as to why we shouldn't serve other in order to preserve our own belongings. He will tell us we shouldn't because it will bring more harm. Perhaps it is that we will become enablers and will mar the integrity of those we seek to serve. He will tell us that we've worked hard for what we have and that others should work hard too.

Satan lies.

Live Worthy

With discernment and humility, we find that God's direction trumps it all. It doesn't matter what the world says, how insignificant or how indulgent the action might seem. God's directive trumps it all.

When He says do, we simply do. When He says don't, we don't.

Therefore, it is imperative that we continually place ourselves under His feet. We seek His foundational Truths. We seek His voice, always and He will answer.

We have seemingly become willing to listen only when His will aligns with our own. We seek His voice only when we have exhausted our own. It is a continual walk. Each breath, each step.

Do we hear His voice, feel His presence?

Seek Him. He is there and the mysteries of the world will unfold. The darkness will begin to dim and His light will shine.

What excuses come to mind when God calls you to serve others? Do you respond readily?

When did you last respond to His call to serve others?

What specific action plan can you take today to live worthy?

His House | 1 Timothy 3:14-15

Although I hope to come to you soon, I am writing you these instructions so that if I am delayed, you will know how people ought to conduct themselves in God's household, which is the church of the living God, the pillar and foundation of the Truth.

How we ought to conduct ourselves in God's household...

There are so many in the world today that have walked away from organized religion, the faith of their parents and God because of their experience in the church. There are churches that have been founded by people who have been mistreated within the church. There are hurting people walking the hallways of the church; all waiting for "the church" to fix itself.

Waiting for the greeter to be friendlier, for the choir to sing better, the Sunday school or Life group teacher to become more personable, the members to become friendlier but what we fail to realize sometimes is that we are the church. All of us.

Yes, there are those who seem more focused in legalism than people. There are those who tend to overlook those they deem unworthy. There are those who speak the Truth on Sunday and dabble with the adversary during the week. This is all true.

But the accountability, the choice lies within each one of us to be obedient where He has called us and sometimes that means being the church amidst the church. It means instead of finding fault, we serve. It means instead of turning our back, we stand firm and obediently allow Him to work through us.

It means becoming the greeter, a voice in the choir, teacher and member.

It means instead of running away we demonstrate to the world the love of Christ. It means being so filled with His Spirit that it overflows from our own while enveloping all who come in our stead.

It means walking worthy in spite of it all.

What a luxury we have to be able to even entertain the thoughts that things should be better. We have brothers and sisters across the world that risk their lives to attend a church gathering. Yet, our attendance has become an afterthought instead of a given. Instead of soaking up the privilege of His Word, satan has taken our freedom and exploited it to lessen its impact in our lives. We critique. We plan our week. We don't engage fully and we might as well not have attended at all.

This is His House.   Live worthy.

What is your greatest complaint regarding the church?

How can you, as part of the church, remedy your greatest complaint?

What specific action plan can you take today to live worthy?

Instead Of God | 1 Timothy 3:16

Beyond all question, the mystery from which true godliness springs is great:

He appeared in the flesh,
was vindicated by the Spirit,
was seen by angels,
was preached among the nations,
was believed on in the world,
was taken up in glory.

It's really quiet simple. He appeared, was seen, preached, believed and was taken up in Glory.

It is what it is.

And, yet, we have made it so much more than that. In our desire to have some form of control, we have created sidebars that extend out from this great mystery. We have taken Christianity from being about Him to being about religion. We have tried to "thicken" the plot of the greatest mystery of all.

We added rules and regulations, judgments and condemnations. What we lack in understanding, we seek to fill with processes and catch phrases. What we lack in our spiritual walk, we fluff with titles, positions and anything that will make us greater, bigger more than.

We judge first and loudly or we judge with the crowd and just loud enough to be included. We follow man-made rules that attempt to keep us in control, rules made for our own good and we seek not for ourselves. But rather we follow man.

Instead of God.

We seek what we can touch in the here and now, instead of the One who created it all. We foster words that carry weight in this earthly world instead of unraveling the greatest mystery of it all.

We garner acceptance and love from a club made of people instead of seeking the only One who can truly grant the membership into Eternity.

And we do all of this, in His name, for His sake.

Who are we?

When it is all stripped away, only the Truth will stand. Only those that have walked the narrow path of righteousness following Him will enter the narrow gate. He came to give us an example and yet many times the example we feel most comfortable following is the Pharisees.

Who are we really following?

When words come out of our mouth are they the same words that Christ would have used? When we encounter someone that the world would condemn, do we follow the world or follow Him?

When this all ends, it will be His face we will encounter not the worlds.

Know who you truly follow. Live worthy.

What is your response when you encounter someone that needs help or that the world would condemn?

How can you respond more as Christ instead of as the world?

What specific action plan can you take today to live worthy?

A Battle For Souls | 1 Timothy 4:1

The Spirit clearly says that in later times some will abandon the faith and follow deceiving spirits and things taught by demons.

Shall we read that again, "Follow deceiving spirits and things taught by demons".

It's a spiritual battle. A battle that is fought every day. A battle that continues into the night and throughout our sleep. A battle for souls.

A battle that plays on the deception within this world. A deception that can appear so pleasing and forthcoming yet at its core is rotten and decaying. A deception that may promote freedom yet lays entrapment. A deceptor that is patient and willing to stalk its prey until the moment of victory lies in reach in the form of a brief moment of weakness, indecisiveness or uncertainty.

A battle for souls.

And while, the destroyer of souls and his demons will stop at nothing to win one more soul away, we oftentimes will focus on one or two that we might win for Christ in our lifetime. Trying not to offend or be offended, we casually live our faith hoping they will take notice. We give Bibles as gifts, worship CDs and nativities, yet do we ever really express the Truth? Have we forgotten what eternity is?

Eternity.

We look at this world and we envision a brighter shinier future. We see trash dumps and children picking for food there and we envision new homes and jobs.

We envision a better place here and a better life now. A life bought and paid for. A life gifted and exchanged. Yet if we aren't careful, we start to invest more in this world than the next. We start to store up for the tomorrows that are uncertain in exchange for an eternity that is.

We try to become god. We try to meet needs that were never ours to meet. We try to step into fixing problems that were never ours to fix. We build a shinier new world that was never ours to build.

And in the face of eternity, none of it will stand. And the deceptors of all deceptors has pulled off the greatest deception of all.

So today, we walk obediently, purposefully and with great discernment knowing that deception is only a moment away. That deception is found in the moment we look away from our Father. So today, we walk steadfastly with our eyes always on Him.

Always.

Where are you trying to fix something for someone instead of sharing Christ with them?

If you knew that it wouldn't be taken offensively, with whom would you share the Gospel?

What specific action plan can you take today to live worthy?

We Will Stand Alone | 1 Timothy 4:2

Such teachings come through hypocritical liars, whose consciences have been seared as with a hot iron.

Maybe they misspoke. Maybe we heard them wrong. Maybe it was taken out of context. Maybe, because to accuse them of being hypocritical liars just wouldn't be politically correct.

So, we make excuses. We look the other way. We give second chances or we walk away so our families won't be negatively impacted by the words being tossed about yet we leave others to fall in their wake. Instead of standing up for Truth, we avoid confrontation at all costs and we protect our own.

Yet, God's Word warns us that this will come. There will be those who will teach deceptively. There will be those who will either knowingly or unknowingly will lead many astray. They will seek to muddy the Truth, to confuse the seekers and to dishearten the faithful and discredit the believers.

And they will do so in such a way, that they will be believed and followed by many.

It is imperative that we know God's Word. In order to know His Word, we must study it as if it were the only Truth in our world today. But, wait a minute, isn't it? Isn't His Word the only foundation that doesn't change from today or tomorrow? A foundation that we can build our lives upon regardless who we are or the circumstances that we find ourselves in. And, yet, we spend so very little time in this Book that is the Living Word.

We spend more time focused on self-help books and other genres that we miss being covered in Our Father's Word. So much so that when we come face to face with cleverly disguised deception, we miss it.

We mistake beautifully decorated large buildings for Truth. We mistake programs and lights for Reality. We fail to see the deception.

Or maybe we choose not to accept the deception.

Because to accept the deception would mean that we would have to change. We would have to take action. We would be held accountable for being part of the deception. But maybe that is the greatest deception of all? We have been led to believe that what we see with our eyes and feel in our hearts is what is real. We have been conditioned that when our physical needs are met then all is well. We have become to believe that it is about what this world offers instead of eternity. If we find success here, we will be okay. If we are okay here, then we are okay. Yet when that final breath comes, it will not matter where we sat in church, whether the pew was cushioned or not or whether our walls were painted. It will simply matter if we believed. Did we choose to follow Him?

Reading throughout scripture, one is hard-pressed to find someone who followed Him and lived happily-ever-after in this world. Trials followed those who believed. They were not promised material or earthly bliss but rather eternal life. What does our life reflect today? What really are we seeking? We can seek happiness here and we may find it. But at what final cost?

When that last day here on this earth comes, those that deceived us will not stand before Him with us. We will stand alone.

May we live worthy.

Where have you let deception continue in your life, your church and your walk?

How much time do you spend daily in His Word, not other books such as this one, but simply His Word?

What specific action plan can you take today to live worthy?

Freedom In Faith | 1 Timothy 4:3

They forbid people to marry and order them to abstain from certain foods, which God created to be received with thanksgiving by those who believe and who know the Truth.

They make rules. Lots of rules. Rules that are intended to guide, to aid and to direct our lives. Under the guise of bringing us closer to Him, they seek to control our lives. Subtly, they weave their way into our homes so that we can begin to lose focus on where God ends and they begin.

They come with authority, positions and titles. Haughty looks and redirection smoothed over with good intentions. They elevate their agendas creating examples for us all to follow. They begin to instruct our way of living from child rearing to marital relations.

Some of them are easily identified by their extreme positions in the governess of daily life. However, the most commonly encountered ones, and perhaps the most dangerous ones, are found walking the aisles of our churches, teaching false doctrine just under the radar confusing new believers

Yet, nowhere is their doctrine of life Biblically sound. It simply isn't.

So, why would we be tempted to follow?

Perhaps, they have created a place that we can physically find acceptance. Like Thomas who needed to touch the wounds on our Christ's hands, sometimes we seek reassurance that we are walking correctly. And we find it here. We find absolutes.

We find not divine direction but precise direction with instant feedback. We find the approval that our fleshy selves so desperately need.

But what we fail to realize is that this earthly approval has absolutely nothing to do with the relationship that our Father wishes to have with us but rather creates an earthly bondage that creates distance between us and our Creator.

We find religion not a relationship. We find a check-off list not a way of life.

I have found my God to be a God of mercy and grace and in that I have found freedom. Freedom from earthly tethers that drain my soul. Freedom that moves mountains.

Freedom that is found in faith not mankind.

What rules govern your life?

How do you know that the rules and standards that you follow are God-given?

What specific action plan can you take today to live worthy?

His Goodness | 1 Timothy 4:4-5

For everything God created is good, and nothing is to be rejected if it is received with thanksgiving, because it is consecrated by the Word of God and prayer.

We are surrounded by God's creation. His goodness.

The food we eat, the provisions He gives, the people in our lives that bring us joy and those that serve to sharpen us have been crafted by His hands. All of it.

Creation made from nothing, brought to being and continuing to be.

Yet, oftentimes we look around our lives and see the decay. We see satan's part and not the Creator's. We find ourselves amidst a broken world, betrayals and hurts, death and sorrows. We fail to see past the deceptor to the Creator, past the destroyer to our Father.

Our eyes stop at what our eyes physical see. Our attention is garnered to what our hearts emotionally feel. Our thoughts too often fall short of the big picture.

A picture that contains so much minute detail that we cannot believe the comprehensiveness of His provisions. A picture that is not bound by time nor space, life nor death. A picture that is pure and powerful.

Satan would have us to believe that this world is it and what an ugly world it has become. He would have us believe that the moment is now, with very little thought of eternity. He would have us believe that our thoughts and feelings are the most important thing in this world coaxing us to lose sight of our soul. We grow more bitter and less patient. We focus on our surroundings and delve into programs and projects. We work faster and harder as time seems to slip through our hands.

All the while, time is passing us by.

God created all of this. It is good. Yes, there are bits of decay and destruction but at the root of it all is His Hand. Even satan bows to the Hand of our Creator. The sooner we accept that this world is not heaven the sooner we will be able to let go of the fantasy that we tend to hold tightly.

This is not it. Sure, we can, and have, created streets of gold. We can make mansions with many rooms and banquets that last for days or weeks at a time. We can "create" heaven on earth. We can make the perfect family, seemingly create the perfect child and search the world wide for our soul mate. We can surround ourselves with "clouds of glory". And with enough money, power and prestige we can have it all.

Until we don't.

Until that moment comes, and it is coming for all of us, that this world becomes a dim reminder of where we used to be. The moment when all of our earthly loot becomes someone else's. The moment when we take that last breath and our heart beats for the very last time. The moment when we exhale and to this world we are no more.

Let us take what He has created and call it good. Let us enjoy it and get great pleasure from it. But let us not be controlled by it. Let our lives be governed with sights on eternity not on the feastings that last for a moment.

Live worthy.

What is your greatest pleasure in this world?

How do you view this world?

What specific action plan can you take today to live worthy?

Truth Is Truth | 1 Timothy 4:6

If you point these things out to the brothers, you will be a good minister of Christ Jesus, bringing up in the truths of the faith and of good teaching that you have followed.

Truth.

It is what it is. It is.

Too many times, we think we need to add to it, explain it or repackage it. Too many times over, it has been added to, explained and repackaged according to other's agendas and motives. So much so, that it seems that truth is debatable, liquid and pliable.

Truth seems to fluctuate within our world today. One person can say the exact same thing as another yet the message is perceived differently. Life can be valuable for one, yet, not for another. Life can be protected for one, yet, not for another. Truth seems to be found in the voice of whoever is talking seemingly as a vapor of water that isn't quite real.

But as a vapor of water, it is real. It does exist regardless whether we can touch it, see it or grasp it.

Truth is Truth. The foundation of Truth never shakes or moves but It stands firm regardless what "we" or "they" say or do. As the experts in our world debate and expound on Truth, the Expert is constant and ever faithful. He will be there when we as this world come face to face with Truth.

We might for a time dabble in a world that allows us to maneuver and manipulate as if there are no absolutes. We have the freedom to create and destroy all in the quest for personal freedoms. We can operate outside the laws of mankind and create new ones when the old ones get in our way. Personal pursuit.

Toiling away day after day crafting our own truth and others just might follow encouraging us as we walk along the path of destruction so eloquently crafted.

But when the trump card is laid down, there is only one Truth. Only one. There will be a moment in time when Truth will be laid down and there will be no argument, no debate, no experts.

Just Truth.

So today, we have a choice. Do we live our lives as if there is only one Truth or do we entertain the thoughts and wiles of many? Do our lives, not our words, but our very lives reflect that?

Live worthy.

What five words describe what you believe to be Truth?

How can you be sure that those that you follow are truly Godly leaders?

What specific action plan can you take today to live worthy?

Train Yourself | 1 Timothy 4:7

Have nothing to do with godless myths and old wives tales; rather, train yourself to be godly.

If doesn't just happen. It is a purposeful, narrowed and directed choice. A daily battle against this world. A daily war against ones flesh.

Sometimes, we look at those that seem to be Godly. Their lives exude the fruits of the Spirit. Their walk with Him is assured and seemingly effortless and we want the relationship that they have.

Perhaps they have such a good relationship because they grew up in the church, perhaps it is because their parents were both Christians, perhaps it was because they married a Christian spouse and the list goes on and on. We struggle to find the factors that are in their life that made their deep and mature relationship with Christ possible. Surely, the reason why our walk with Christ is so different is because they've been given something that we haven't and this gets us off the hook. Completely.

For if we look deeper into their world instead of looking at the superficial material blessings, we might find the Truth. These people have struggled and wrestled as we have, however, the difference in us has been their response. When God felt far away, they didn't complain and commiserate with others who felt the same; they took action to place themselves in His work. When they were living lives of blessing and blessing, they didn't coast or forget about Who blessed them, they used that time to strengthen their faith through prayer and the study of His Word. And when the valleys and trenches of life came their way, they stood tall in the faith that He had already overcome whatever trial they were facing.

The people who exude true faith are those who live and breathe it every moment of every day their faith.

In a world that is filled with explanations upon explanations, myths and wives tales that we believe simply because someone told us or we believe because a part of us is afraid not to follow them because what if it is true, we must decide in our mind not to dabble there. Either we believe or we don't. Either Christ is real or He's not. We can't continue to entertain both sides of the camp. I can't place my trust in Him for my future and continue to scan my horoscope for my direction. I can't trust my child's life with Him and still pay my respects to the idol that will people say will protect him on this earth. We can't live confused. We either do or we don't.

So we train our minds to be centered only on Truth not even to entertain thoughts that are contrary. Now, the world will say that this is narrow- minded and judgmental contrasting what our Father told us "not to have anything to do with godless myths and old wives tales". Which do we choice to follow?

It's a choice.

What superstitions do you still hold onto, just in case?

What do you need to rid your life of in order to focus fully on Him?

What specific action plan can you take today to live worthy?

Real Food | 1 Timothy 4:8

For physical training is of some value, but godliness has value for all things, holding promise for both the present life and the life to come.

Real Food. Low Carb. High Carb. More Water. High Protein. Low Fat.

When we are committed to get in better physical shape whether it be to adhering to a physician's advice or be it due to a cruise schedule in mid-winter, the quest to eat appropriately becomes part of our every thought. From the time we awake, we plan what we can and can't eat. We watch every morsel that that goes into our body. We count, weigh and choose based on the goodness that each decision will bring. We choose to put off instant gratification in order to obtain a longer lasting pleasure. Slowly, but assuredly as we persevere, we find that our decisions make the next choices easier to make until before we know it we are making healthy choices easier than before. Our hard work and discipline pays off.

But what about our spiritual lives? Our quest for Godliness? Does it encompass our every thought? Do we mull over every thought that comes into our lives? Do we reject, quickly, those we know we should? Do we plan, count and measure so that we might be strengthened by Him?

It seems in this world that we have become very complacent regarding our spiritual training. For those that have stepped up and entered the ring, so to speak, they find themselves criticized and called radical instead of encouraged.

We have forgotten that physical strength, while it may provide for us well in the here and now, will not be the source of our strength through our greater trials.

Our bodies will experience the decay and destruction of the world. Some of us will encounter injury and disease head-on. Others will slowly age and watch the decline of their youth. However, faith as it is strengthened provides a hope that is not of this world. It is preventative at its very core. As we mature, instead of it breaking down, our faith grows stronger.

As we strive toward Godliness, as our faith deepens, we find ourselves with a faith that is unshakeable. So that when trials and tribulations come our way, we don't even hear the whispered lies of satan, but rather feel the Holy presence of our Father and experience His indescribable peace. When our physical world crashes amongst us, we don't feel the tragedy yet revel in Whose we are for eternity. Our physical strength is but a speck in the sand compared to the strength of Our Father.

So then why do we overlook the source of our greatest strength? We are a world that places great value and worth upon physical prowess and appearance yet we discount the Creator from which it flows. Perhaps it comes from the pursuit of being in control or reaching for a prize that is tangible and visible for our eyes to see. We train for 5ks and marathons. Long and short runs followed by stretching becomes a part of who we are. We purchase running shoes and plan our routes with great care and discernment. And while, all of this is good, do we train just as hard for our spiritual journey?

See the battle, while not always visible, is continuous. It exists in the spiritual realm without ceasing. Soldiers would never walk into battle without training and being prepared for the engagement that they will soon face.

Yet, everyday we engage in spiritual battle from what our eyes see and our ears hear. Our lives are surrounded. Yet, many of us are ill-prepared. We find ourselves confused, tired, disheartened and despondent at the end of each day. No hope. No grace. No mercy. We know the words exist but we don't feel them in our lives. We appear to be beat up by this world just as much, or more so, than whose who do not believe.

So today, focus on your spiritual training. Make a plan. Make it a priority. Take as much care in its execution as that of the greatest diet or exercise plan of all time. In the end, it will be the only thing that matters.

Live worthy.

What does your spiritual "exercise plan" look like?

Where is your focus found as you plan out your day?

What specific action plan can you take today to live worthy?

"I'm Just Not Good Enough" | 1 Timothy 4:9-10

This is a trustworthy saying that deserves full acceptance (and for this we labor and strive), that we put our hope in the living God, who is the Savior of all men, and especially of those who believe.

It is a hard life. A difficult life. The ladies that we serve that live on the borders of the city dump raise their families in an area of desperation. A place where there is never enough for everyone so you must scrap and fight to make sure you are at the front of every line. Food found today must be eaten and used today for if left for tomorrow it increases the likelihood that one will be robbed. A place where even the youngest learns quickly how to fight in order to protect oneself. Women and young girls are preyed upon. A place where happiness is a rarity at any age. They dig through the trash everyday. All day, they dig in search of anything of value or worth such as plastic, cardboard, metal or food then they set it on fire in hopes of finding any metal that they might have missed. Young and old, babies on hips or toddlers milling through the city's discarded waste they search every day for that day's needs.

They know what they do. They know where they are on the world's list of hierarchy. They know. They aren't innately happy or even the least bit satisfied by seemingly their lot in life. No one dreamed of living here but by life's circumstances they ended up here. A place where they are looked down upon. A place where they feel lesser than. A place where there is seemingly no hope.

And as satan weaves his lies even here, we find the universal thought that "I'm just not good enough" or "I have to clean up first". No, my God says, "Come as you are." But that's the clincher, we have to come. We have to make that step, that choice, that decision to say, " yes".

We come as we are problems and all. We come with open hands to the only One that make bring joy into our world accompanied by a peace that this world will never understand. We simply come for we are all His. Each and every one.

And after we come, we lay down the ways of this world. With eyes on our Father, we find a new way. We find that joy is not found in what we own or possess but rather in Whom we place our trust. We find that Hope isn't dependent upon our financial security or net worth but rather in what He sees in us. We find that days that we once filled with activities and programs, days that we were exhaustive in the end yet rarely satisfied, are days now filled with a newfound purpose.

His purpose. A purpose with a bigger plan in place. Something bigger than ourselves. A purpose that satan may try to mess with but with God at helm, the storms can be weathered.

In the blink of an eye, God could change the poverty of this world. He could. But I have learned that the answer isn't about material worth or gain, for some of the most impoverished may live in the most beautiful of mansions. Some of the most impoverished may possess the greatest riches of this world.

Live Worthy

May God open our eyes to see what He sees to see the reality of this world. To see past the facade whether it be mounds of trash or mounds of gold. To see Truth. May we care more about our fellow man's soul than his net worth. May we step out in faith to those that surround us. May our lives be a direct reflection of His joy and peace.

When you look out upon this world, what do you see?

Where do you stand spiritually? Are your rich or impoverished?

What specific action plan can you take today to live worthy?

Command And Teach | 1 Timothy 4:11

Command and teach these things.

It doesn't just happen. Just as we must train our spiritual life, we must also take care to command and teach others. So many times we look at others' lives and we either don't want to get involved or we choose to look the other way because it looks too messy, will take too much time or whatever other excuse that we can find to stay focused on our own journey and not take command of others and as a result, we find a world that is disconnected and disillusioned.

Our neighbors, while they once were our greatest source of fellowship and help, have become an endless sea of nondescript faces. Our co-workers, while once considered family has become our competition. Our fellow members at church while once considered brothers and sisters have become names and photos on a roster. Satan continues to take our greatest relationships and attempts to lessen our intimacy. Intimacy that reaches deep and creates accountability morphing into relationships that weather storms together. We are a people that should never walk alone. In addition to our Heavenly Father, we have sisters and brothers that we been given to walk this journey with us. Not alone.

Satan tries to convince us that no one cares. He weaves a web of lies that would tells us that if they knew the truth then they would leave us. And the longer we keep ourselves alone in his darkness then the more alone we feel, the more despair we experience and the longer we feel isolated from the Light within this world.

Then his lies can really take root. We isolate ourselves further and believe all the lies that our head contains so that when someone does reach through the barriers we have constructed, we immediately distrust their motives. We assume that everyone has an agenda that is focused on their own benefit and our demise.

Yet, what would happened if we chose to be different than the current status quo? What if we reach beyond knowing our neighbor and actual love on them? What if we began to look at our colleagues as family and encourage them to be the best they can be? What if when we reached across the pews to shake hands we allowed our eyes to connect to each others' souls? What if we called satan's lies what they are?

We all have a past. We all have current issues. We all live in a decaying world. When our daughter passed away, one of the most comforting measures we received was when those who had walked the journey before us reached out to us.

They took their pain and were willing to relive quite possibly the darkest day of their lives in order to walk beside us during ours. They gave us hope not with their words but with their presence.

The Bible, His Words, is more than just words on a page. They are a call to action. A call to move. A call to really live the lives we were meant to live. It is a choice, maybe not the easiest one initially, but it comes with the most eternal of rewards. Why aren't we moving?

Live worthy.

What are your neighbors' greatest challenges in life?

How much time do you spend praying for them and theirs?

What specific action plan can you take today to live worthy?

Walk In Joy | 1 Timothy 4:12

Don't let anyone look down on you because you are young, but set an example for the believers in speech, in conduct, in love, in faith and in purity.

Set an example. Not for the unbelieving world but for the believers.

While we will experience mountaintops and valleys on our journey in this world, and some of the valleys may seem longer than the mountaintops, we will learn that joy isn't determined by where we are in our circumstances but rather where we are in our faith in Him. We serve a God who moves mountains, calms the sea and has raised the dead. He, himself, conquered death. Shouldn't we be excited about this? Shouldn't this alone be reason for pure and uncontainable joy? But, yet, we seem to accept that even this joy will wane. We come to expect the new-found joy in new believers to decrease. We warn them against burn-out. We advise them to pace themselves. Instead of finding ourselves caught up in their energy, we too often sit back telling ourselves that they, too, will become like us. That we've seen this before and soon they will settle down and join the rest of the ranks on the pews.

Soon they will "mature".

Their goofy smiles will settle back to quick head nods. Their wild and abandoned embraces will return to a hand-shake. Their attendance will decrease from every time the doors are open to normal attendance.

Their constant chatter about Christ will finally return to sports, news and weather and we can't stop feeling uncomfortable around them because they remind us of once the uncontainable joy that we felt ourselves.

Some how, some where within our own walks, we begin to look upon earthly things to satisfy our souls. We look toward relationships, progress and material wealth. We strive for peace, love and the calming of our spirit within.

We search for normal. And when we come up empty-handed, we become disheartened and disillusioned. We let ourselves be convinced that God is far way, that He doesn't care and we feel our excitement falter. The people within the church who doted on us as they were sharing the Truth no longer even have time to have coffee with us. Satan begins to weave the lies that no one cares now that they have added another mark to their membership and we watch as they start to court the new attendees.

And this is where we start to tread on water instead of standing firm.

We start to look upon the people that surround us to justify our faith. We start to rely on the relationships that God placed around us to encourage us in our journey towards faith instead of using them as the purpose in which they were intended. They were never intended to take the place of our quest for Our Father and, yet, they do. We begin to lose our joy and excitement. Some of us will falter completely and will stop attending church and reading our Bibles all together. Others will stay, albeit disgruntled, but will stay. We will follow the examples of those before us, carry the hurt in our hearts and will find ourselves finding fault in the things that surround us whether it be the carpet, the music, the pastor.

Our physical needs are not being met, and we believe the lie that once they are met then our lives will be good. A few will become what some might would call "radical". The joy never decreases, yet, seems to be replenished each day anew. Regardless of the circumstances that life seems to throw their way, they walk in the assured foundation that He is Lord and that is enough for them.

Though, people may try to discourage them, believers even, may try to remind them of the realities of this world, they live for their place in eternity daily walking with Him.

For their faith is not dependent on anything of this world.

What example does our daily lives set for those that surround us? Do we walk with the joy of the Lord? It is ours, as believers, for the taking and, yet, too many times we let the world snatch from our hands or we willingly give it away.

It is a choice how we decide to live, how we decide to face each and every day. Do we live as those who are forgiven? Do we live as those who serve the King? Do we live as a child of God should live? Our lives should be an example, not just to the world, but believers who have seemingly lost their joy. Through our daily walk, through our words, actions and relationships, the joy that God has given us should overflow into the lives of those around us.

It is okay to be happy. It is.

For the joy that we have, is a joy that has been given from the King and that joy shouldn't be hidden but rather lived.

Live worthy. Always.

Do you live a joyful life?

How do you encourage new believers?

What specific action plan can you take today to live worthy?

Time. It Takes Time | 1 Timothy 4:13

Until I come, devote yourself to the public reading of Scripture, to preaching and to teaching.

An investment to take from our own lives and devote to others. We wonder where the harvest is and why it hasn't come. We look in frustration at the youth of today, those that are different than us and the world. We shake our heads at "what this world is coming to" and voice our dismay.

What if, however, there is a correlation to the amount of time that we, as believers, dedicate to reading, preaching and teaching and the state of affairs that this world is in today?

Is there?

Have we, as children of God, fallen into the trappings of this world so heavily that we have missed our opportunities? Have we been so deceived that we have forgotten that they are ours to begin with? Not the church's, not the staffs but ours.

Until He returns, and this is what we shall do until He returns, we should have total devotion of ourselves to Him and His Kingdom.

Reading, preaching and teaching.

Yet, so much of our days are spent on everything else. Activities fill our calendars crowding our true purposes. We focus on being successful and secure in a world that was never meant to provide a firm foundation.

Between our personal endeavors and that of our children, we invest so heavily in this world and so minimally in eternity.

So minimally as if to just get by.

If we really want to see the harvest, we have to be willing to set aside some of our own personal agendas and submit to His.

We have 24 hours in a day. That's it. No more. No less. How we choose to spend that time will reflect our true intentions. We may talk a good talk but our day-in and day-out walk will reflect what we truly have sat our allegiance toward.

The day will come when He will return. He will. Minimal, is that what we really want to bring to the table? This is not a game in which we have a scorekeeper but rather life that either ends in eternal life or eternal hell.

Live worthy.

Does your spiritual growth receive as much attention as other worldly endeavors?

Are you simply to busy? How can you adjust your schedule?

What specific action plan can you take today to live worthy?

"But I Want That One" | 1 Timothy 4:14

Do not neglect your gift, which was given to you through prophetic message when the body of elders laid hands on you.

We may not vocalize it as we might have when we were kids. We might not even completely realize when we do it. We watch others when they are "in their element" and we want that, too. We want to be in our element. We want that feeling of being where we created to be.

And we can be.

But only when we stop neglecting the gifts that He has given us. Only when we stop trying to emulate other people's lives.

But, oh how wonderful would it be to be able to _____. Fill in the blank. We've all had those moments when we see someone serving, someone worshipping, someone speaking or praying and it is incredible. "I want that." So much so that we tend to forget the gifts that we have because, well quite frankly, they aren't as flashy. The gifts that we have aren't the gifts and talents that lend to being out in front, that receives accolades and recognition. Sometimes they are the gifts that happen in the dark of night such as praying while others sleep. Or maybe cleaning and washing while preparing for others to come. Maybe it is to just be.

We all know that there are many parts to the body of Christ. We all have heard it and understand the concept but do we really buy into it? And buy into it with the teeth that says, "I'll do my part regardless what it is."

What if your part becomes emptying the trash cans? Are you okay with that? Are you okay with it when someone of seemingly lesser statue takes your place at the lead?

It's a humble walk.

A walk that is completely contrary to what this world understands. A walk that says I will walk first when needed and last when needed realizing that regardless of earthly position the journey is the same.

It is the walk of obedience and it will take us on a path that He has ordained. Not for the faint of heart. Not for the accolades of this world but for His purpose.

And on that path, we seemingly find that the journey was orchestrated perfectly for each one of us to grow us, to mature us and to prepare us. We learn that each of us has been given what we need to set foot on His path. The gifts He's given me is for my journey not for yours. As, yours is not for mine. And if I nurture my gifts with discipline and steadfast devotion to Him, I can find that it doesn't matter what everyone else has. It doesn't matter at all. In fact, we will no longer see our differences, as satan so incredulously tends to point out, but we begin to see the tapestry of God's people.

We see the church with no one color of thread more vibrant than the other but rather each fulfilling the purpose they created to fill.

Live worthy.

What talents within the church do you wish you had?

When do you feel that you are most at ease with yourself?

What specific action plan can you take today to live worthy?

Be Diligent | 1 Timothy 4:15

Be diligent in these matters; give yourself wholly to them, so that everyone may see your progress.

Be diligent. Give yourself wholly.

It's pretty clear, isn't it? He desires all of us. Every single bit. Not just the part that appears for the school drop- off or Sunday church but the part of ourselves that no one even sees.

Wholly.

The part of ourselves that feels unworthy, distant from others and small. The part of ourselves that struggles to get out of bed. The part of us that yells at our kids and walk quickly away before the rage takes over. Even that part.

He's a big God.

He can handle it all. He refines us and makes us whole again. But in order for Him to be able to do that, we have to be willing to surrender ourselves to Him even the parts that no ones sees.

We have to trust Him.

Trust that He won't turn us away. Trust that He won't hurt us. Trust that He will not turn His back on us. He may be our only hope but He's not an unworthy hope. He is the hope that will transcend our lives. We find ourselves holding tighter to what we know, yet, if we would just let go; He would fill us to the point of overflowing with joy.

Isn't that what we want?

We want fulfillment. A life worthy. We want to be a part of something bigger than ourselves. And then there are some days that we just want to survive. Days when we have no more to give to anyone. Days when we are surrounded always by some one wanting something and we are, oh, so limited.

But He isn't. He can do all things. We just have to surrender and let Him work. We have to be diligent in becoming who we will be. Diligent in protecting our hearts and minds. We have to trust that He will lead only where we should go. As long as our eyes stay on Him, we will not falter.

The worlds will tells us that it is too much for us to handle. That it should break our hearts but these are just lies that satan weaves. When we walk fully focused on Him we will rest in His arms.

Diligent.

Live worthy.

What lies does satan tell you?

What promises of God's do you have yet to claim?

What specific action plan can you take today to live worthy?

Realness | 1 Timothy 4:16

Watch your life and doctrine closely. Persevere in them, because if you so, you will save yourself and your hearers.

Know what you devote yourself to.

Christianity is more than a fad, a club or an efficient networking group. Christianity is based on our individual relationship with the living God. It is real.

When we bow our heads in prayer, we pray to the One Almighty. When we join in worship, we worship the King of Kings.

Real.

And yet, somewhere, we have lost the realness, the reverence and the awestruckness of the Almighty. We go through the motions like everyone else. We attend all the required events and pray at meal times. But all too often, it is by rote memory and not from our very souls.

And then we wonder why we aren't being fed. We wonder where He is. Oh, we claim He shows up now and again but we fail to recognize that it is ourselves who tend to only show up now and again.

He is always there. Always.

Much as due diligence changes when one holds a water gun and then a loaded real gun, where does our diligence stand when we come before our Heavenly Father? Do we live our lives honoring Him without ceasing? Do we realize just how real He is? Do we understand the implications that come with saying I am a believer and I will follow Him.

For some, that means walking a completely different path than you initially dreamed. For others, that means finding joy amidst destruction. For us all, it means living a life of obedience seeking Him above all things.

Praying, reading His Word, worshipping, loving and forgiving in a way that will look radically different from the world.

Watch ourselves.

We live as if our time here on the earth will never end. We live as if we have our whole lives ahead of us to "get it right". So we live for today focusing on schedules and deadlines all the while missing those that God has sent to us. We run from here to there accomplishing tons of worldly things and we forget to sharpen the only tool in our world that really matters.

Do you know Whose you are?

How do you encourage new believers?

What specific action plan can you take today to live worthy?

Family | 1 Timothy 5:1-2

Do not rebuke an older man harshly, but exhort him as if he were your father. Treat younger men as brothers, older women as mothers, and younger women as sisters, with absolute purity.

Unfortunately, in light of today's world, this is all relative. We live in a world in which each new generation seems to claim equal respect regardless of age or gender. Family dynamics are overall at best variable and family lines are all over the place.

A world where children kill their parents and each other. A world where parents don't protect those they have been given. A world where the value of life seems to vary from state to state. A world that says, "I will consider your needs as long as it doesn't infringe upon mine."

Me, first.

My needs. My wants. My desires.

At any cost.

Even the cost of our very souls. We seem to be able to tolerate the evil that surrounds us as long as it doesn't come close to our tent. We can turn the other way, push it out of our minds and not even consider the ramifications as long as we, ourselves, are not involved or, at least, we aren't publicly acknowledged as being involved.

But can we really be okay with this? The Bible is as relevant today as it was the moment the ink began to dry on its first print.

Relevant regardless whether or not we choose to be obedient and follow. Its relevance does not depend on our willingness to follow. It doesn't.

But the work place is a dog eat dog world regardless of the person's age or gender. It's either get with the program or get out. If you mess with the bull, you get the horns.

Really?

We might "win" in the workplace that next position or title. We might even push out those that God placed in our path because they weren't able "to cut the mustard" anymore or because the conviction was so strong inside is that we had to push them away.

God's Word is for everywhere, every place and every time. There are no what-ifs or loopholes. It is what it is.

The elderly man that struggles with technology, help him. The older woman that you see every day, show her kindness. The beautiful young girl that pops up on your computer screen, turn it off. The young man searching for validation, help him find it in Christ before he finds it in the world. Don't encourage the evil. Reach beyond the trappings of this world and live each day for the Kingdom to come.

It won't look pretty, probably will cost us a few 'friends' and maybe that position we've been vying for but the "Well done, good and faithful one" will erase all of that.

Live worthy. Be different.

What does your work "persona' reveal about yourself?

How can you demonstrate the love of Christ to those in which you daily engage?

What specific action plan can you take today to live worthy?

Widows | 1 Timothy 5:3

Give proper recognition to those widows who are really in need.

It is easy when we get busy to forget. We begin to pray when we first hear the news. We take food, attend visitation and the funeral. We stay close prepared to help with anything.

And then, we forget.

We don't mean to. We have the best intentions but life gets busy. We become engrossed in our own world that their loss falls to the back of our minds. We lose touch.

And then we remember.

By this time, weeks and months have past by. In all honesty, it is almost embarrassing to contact them now. What will say? Awkward at its very best. We don't want to cause them to relive the pain or hurt especially if they are doing better so we don't make contact and we say a quick prayer promising ourselves that we will do better next time.

And satan wins.

He has successfully isolated the one who grieves by strategically weaving lies surrounding the very ones who should bring comfort. He attempts to immobilize the church in the grief process.

And our widows stand-alone.

We are called to be His hands and feet. We are called to take action. It might feel awkward and make us uncomfortable as satan tries to discourage that first step. But step out anyway. We may be met with tears or dry eyes and that's okay. The purpose is that we be obedient to the commands He has given.

Think of whom we know that are widows. Their needs will vary greatly. Some will simply need a listening ear or a hug. Others may need physical protection from the evils of this world. Some perhaps need help with small repairs and others the provision of food. Regardless of the material necessities, the message is the same, "You are loved. Not forgotten but loved."

Live worthy.

Who are the widows in your life?

How can you follow God's direction to care for them? (If you don't know any, how can you meet one?

What specific action plan can you take today to live worthy?

He Did | 1 Timothy 5:4

But if a widow has children or grandchildren, these should learn first of all to put their religion into practice by caring for their own family and so repaying their parents and grandparents, for this is pleasing to God.

Put our religion into practice. Where the rubber meets road. Walk the talk.

We can spend our whole lives studying, reflecting and disciplining ourselves to be well learned in God's Word and completely miss the whole purpose. Jesus, Himself, is the perfect example of Truth put into action. He not only gave us His Word but He put a realness behind that action that is second to none.

He not only said to welcome the children. He welcomed them.

He not only said to love. He loved.

The only person who had ever walked this earth who had the true authority to preach excessively to the masses did more than just impart words. He imparted love. Love to a world that was starving for real love.

A world very similar to our world today. A world that needs compassion and empathy. A world that is searching to be relevant somewhere, in some way. A world that oftentimes sees religion as pure judgment and hypocrisy instead of love. A world that tends to see the church as a cliché instead of a haven for all who come.

A world in which many Christians are struggling just as much as unbelievers are struggling. So much so, that we have very little to give. We have very little to offer when someone is placed upon our path. With only enough energy to finish our personal day, we turn inward careful not to become involved.

Yet, it is here where Christ will be most evident. In the place where we can give no more, Christ will give through us.

Unfortunately, we pull the ripcord before we ever can see what He can do. We call 'uncle' in a world where 'uncle' doesn't stop the game but rather changes the players.

If we could only give ourselves the grace to say, "Can't do it. But He can and I trust Him enough to know He will."

In the end, we all know the words, He wins. That's the end of the game. Yet, we still play the game of life as those who don't believe His ending do.

We play it safe.

How different might we live if we truly lived as if we believed the ending? Much as a player in a basketball game who knows that in the end his team will win, the fouls, bad calls and poor sportsmanship wouldn't matter as much because when the buzzer rings his team wins.

When the "buzzer" rings here, God wins the rest is just noise. The betrayal, the sadness, the sickness, the disappointment, the craziness and the list goes on and on. There are fouls made in this world that will not count toward the final score. The final score is settled.

But rather, they will shape us into who we are. Will we be bitterly shaped or sharpened? Will we fall or stand? Will we love greatly or ration it out?

Live worthy.

What are the fouls that have occurred in your life?

How can you let them shape you instead of slight you?

What specific action plan can you take today to live worthy?

Pure Obedience | 1 Timothy 5:5-6

The widow who is really in need and left all alone puts her hope in God and continues night and day to pray and to ask God for help. But the widow who lives for pleasure is dead even while she lives.

Where do we start? Who do we help? How do we know where we can make the greatest impact as opposed to creating more harm?

We serve a sovereign God. A God that is personal and relevant every moment of every day. A God that in the blink of an eye can change the world. A God that in a heartbeat can transform a life.

Our part is to play our part. Whatever that might be. We must be obedient. Within the fleeting of His thoughts, He could change the lives of those who are considered the poorest of the poor. He doesn't need us at all but rather He allows us to be a part.

We look at those less fortunate than us and immediately our minds are concerned with how do we make this better or at least prettier? How can we clean this up? And sometimes, God impresses upon us that is precisely what we should do. And sometimes, He says to be still and watch Him at work. While other times, He instructs us to love greatly right where they are changing nothing but being His hands and feet.

Satan will try to turn it into something more confusing than it actually is. He will encourage us to move mountains that God had ordained to stay. He will pluck at our emotions and then come back and poke at our pride when our best intentions wane results that fail to meet our expectations. And we become disillusioned and discouraged, walking away from the very call that He has sent us.

Every step, every gesture is an act of pure obedience.

The more we walk in obedience to Him the more distinct His voice becomes and the more real our motives evolve. As we begin to see through His eyes and not the world's, we see through the lenses of eternity instead of the here and now.

We see promise amidst the chaos. We see life where the dead lie. We see hope instead of the hopeless.

When we choose to walk in obedience to Him above all else, we find it's not about the outcome but rather the journey. We lay it down as sacrifice and rest in the peace of having completed our part. Our portion. We stop overthinking, over-feeling and overanalyzing and we begin to fully trust Him.

Live Worthy

What do you see around you today?

What is God asking you to do with what you see? What is His plan, not your own?

What specific action plan can you take today to live worthy?

We Are The Messenger | 1 Timothy 5:7

Give the people these instructions, too, so that no one may be open to blame.

Maybe I should say it, but I don't know how they will take it. Maybe I'll talk to them tomorrow or perhaps next week. Maybe someone else will say something. I know, I know, I should but I'm _____. (scared, worried, hesitant, too busy)

We've all had those times when we know God is impressing upon us to say something. Not the times when our flesh is screaming within us to say something but rather those times when the gentle Spirit of God presses us to talk to someone and we don't. We know that the message is ours to take. We know it is from God and yet, we hesitate. We put off the inevitable. We wait. We play games with time and place. (If God really wants us to talk with them, they will be at the corner when I come to the stoplight...in the middle of the night.)

It doesn't even have to be something too terribly important. Sometimes it is the simply greeting of just wanting to share fellowship while other times it is sharing with them our relationship with our Father in Heaven, the greatest news of all, and we choke. We wait for someone else to do it. Someone who has been "properly" trained. Someone who has been "through the course". Anyone, but us. We watch for God to put people in their path who can talk to them. Often times, we even finagle people in their path so that the message can be told.

Yet, we are the messenger.

What if the message is merely to say affirm to them that someone has been praying for them? Or maybe a message of encouragement to help them through their journey?

And left to us, the messenger is mute.

Are we afraid? Are we afraid that maybe we haven't heard God right?

That maybe, just maybe, we will walk up to them and say what we are to say and they will look at us like we are absolutely crazy. Has this ever happened to any of us? When have we ever heard direction from our Father, acted upon it and been led astray? Rather, have we had His voice reaffirmed time and time again when we choose to be obedient to His call? And, quite possibly, we have also had His voice affirmed again and again when we fail to speak in a timely manner and the opportunity passes us by and we know by the feeling in the pit of our stomach that we missed our part.

Perhaps it was regarding a marriage in trouble, a life caught off-balance or the end of this life, as we know it. Regardless of the circumstances, the result is the same, we allowed ourselves to become too caught up in worldly emotion to carry out heavenly words.

God uses each of us in so many ways. We just have to listen closely and act. Be obedient.

Live worthy.

When have you let God's message pass you by?

What is God asking you to do today?

What specific action plan can you take today to live worthy?

Family | 1 Timothy 5:8

If anyone does not provide for his relatives, and especially for his immediate family, he has denied the faith and is worse than an unbeliever.

And this then is how we should live.

But why is it so incredibly difficult? We live in a world that has been corrupted by sin. A world that has pitted fathers against sons, mothers against daughters and siblings against siblings. A world in which satan prowls seeking for opportunity to cause despair and to destroy. And then he paints the perfect picture of what a real "family" should look like further dashing salt into an already hemorrhaging wound.

So, we try harder. We try to anticipate what is needed. We try to create, at the very least, the picture of family that we see in our minds. We participate in family gatherings; bring food and presents focusing on the weather while praying inside that we can just make it through without causing or witnessing a blowup in epic fashion. And when we do, we agree that we are family and so we continue on in the same pattern because, of course, we are family.

And the insane cycle continues.

Instead of being loved unconditionally and protected by those given to us in family, we may be hurt and stripped of all love and dignity. Instead of being completed and fulfilled by our family, we walk away scarred and abused. Instead of being built up, we may be kicked down.

So, we walk away disillusioned and hurt.

Or quite possibly the opposite, maybe we are surrounded by a family that offers everything material processions yet foregoing our emotional needs. Or maybe we are in a family that has agreed to disagree and lives as strangers and apart.

How many times do we go back? How many times do we get hurt? How many times does our heart have to break?

Our freedom comes from Christ. In Him alone. We will never find fulfillment in another person or group of people and if we do, we need to beware of whom we are following. We will find who we truly are only in Him. Looking towards Him, full face, we will find guidance in light of the cross instead of our worldly desires.

Each journey, we will find will be different. My path different from yours, yet, guided by the same One. Through discernment, we may find that we need to step up and be more of a physical presence or quite possibly that we need to step down and love from afar.

It doesn't matter what it looks like in my eyes or your eyes. It is how it resounds to our Father that is important.

His guidance. Live worthy.

What do you desire to be different in your family?

Where is God calling you to respond to others as part of the church family?

What specific action plan can you take today to live worthy?

So They Watch | 1 Timothy 5:9-10

No widow may be put on the list of widows unless she is over sixty, has been faithful to her husband, and is well known for her good deeds, such as bringing up children, showing hospitality, washing the feet of the saints, helping those in trouble and devoting herself to all kinds of good deeds.

There are qualifications. Actions. Limits.

A minimum requirement, so to speak.

Many times the world sees the extension of love from the church as the people within being naive. They see people being helped and they laugh as the members within are being taken advantage of. They witness as "free food" is distributed and shake their heads as they see what the world sees---a free meal. They participate in distributions and revel in the craziness of what others would give to people they don't even know.

How crazy could they possibly be?

Crazy enough to follow a King who turned away from keeping court with the world's elite and invested in those who were truly seeking the Kingdom. Crazy enough to forgo the trappings of this world in anticipation of eternity in the next. Crazy enough to say, "it's not about me but rather obedience to the King."

Because of obedience to Him, we can withstand rumors weaved in hopes that we might falter. Because of His grace, we can react different than this world would expect us to react. Because of His mercy, we can stand while others might fall. Because of His forgiveness, we can forgive when the hurt is seemingly unforgivable.

The world won't understand. Not at all. It will watch and wait. It will peer close enough to see that there is a difference and wonder. It will react sometimes defensively to hurt first and, yet, when the last sword falls, love will still abound.

And this is where we come in; we are an extension of His love here on this earth. We might face criticism both real and made-up. We may face our greatest fears as the world stands by and waits to see the failing of our God. As we hand over our last to a known swindler, the world laughs and judges harshly.

However within the world, there are those that are watching closer than the majority. In their hearts, they recognize a difference and within their souls and they are intrigued.

So they watch.

We must live in such a way that when the world watches we stand ready with an explanation as to why. They may not understand. The contrast will be great but those who are being called will ask. We must be ready to give our personal testimony with love and intensity that comes only from Him and Him alone.

Live ready.

Who do you observe throughout your day that makes you wonder?

What would someone observing you today see?

What specific action plan can you take today to live worthy?

"It is Yours For the Taking" | 1 Timothy 5:11

As for younger widows, do not put them on such a list. For when their sensual desires overcome their dedication to Christ, they want to marry.

When our desires overcome our dedication to Christ...

We all try hard with the best intentions. Every Sunday, every Easter, every revival, every new dedication to Him we intend to maintain the close relationship that we experience. We truly do.

And then life happens.

The week starts and with each week comes challenges anew. A new job starts that comes with new things to learn. Or maybe nothing new happens but rather a continuation of the world as we have created it to be. A world filled. Filled with everything we can possibly fill it with. Classes and more classes, activities, meetings, multicolored, tabbed events that plan out our week. A week that leaves us tired before we even begin.

But we are completely dedicated to Him, yes?

God desires to be present in every moment of our lives. Every moment. Not just during church on Sunday, not just during our devotion time, not just before we eat our food but every moment dedicated to Him. His glory.

And what would that look like? How would our lives look differently?

Quite possibly we would purposefully choose to live more intentional with the knowledge that every action, every action that we take on this earth contributes either positively or negatively toward the Kingdom. Maybe, we would seek out relationships that empower us instead of bind us. Instead of living days filled with monotony, we would live lives filled with adventure and purpose.

Oh, satan will tell us the opposite. That a life filled with Christ is a life wasted. A boring life filled with drudgery and judgment. A life that we aren't worthy to live. A life that only the "perfect" deserve.

And God says it is yours for the taking.

We shouldn't be afraid to say, " I'm all in." We shouldn't be hesitant to set boundaries and barriers to protect our relationship with God in order to nurture it. It doesn't take tragedy for us to feel God's hand. It is always there. Always. It is us who pull away caught up in our world instead of purposefully staying next to Him.

Twenty-four hours in a day. How much time do we spend walking with our Father. We are called to pray without ceasing, daily communion with the One who saved us all.

And then when temptation comes our way, our flesh will not falter but rather will stand firm on the foundation that has been built upon.

Live worthy.

When did you last feel close to God?

As you look throughout your life, what were the times that you felt closest to Him?

What specific action plan can you take today to live worthy?

Judgment | 1 Timothy 5:12

Thus they bring judgment on themselves, because they have broken their first pledge.

They bring judgment on themselves.

There are consequences. There are. Drop a glass vase on a concrete floor and it more than likely will break. Turn a full cup upside down and it will spill. Yes?

Just like in our own lives every day we make choices to live as we choose to live. We can choose whichever way we wish. Free will and all. We love free will. The ability to make our own choices, design our own lives and forge our own path.

It's when we forge into a trail of thorns that we begin to grumble and call foul. The moment our free will selves anchors in on extreme delightfulness instead of discipline and we find ourselves deeper than we realized we could go that we cry out in pain and agony.

How unbelievably unfair.

When we push doors open that weren't ready to be opened, when we seek where we should never tread or when we dabble just close enough to revel in the heat of the fire, we exercise the greatest gift we've ever been given to fulfill our own worldly desires. We tell ourselves that it is okay.

We explain it away using God many times as our conspirator. "If He allows it, then it must be okay." "If she follows me, it is meant to be." "Maybe God provided him to me to help ease my struggles in my marriage."

Just because we can doesn't mean we should.

There is another force working in this world. A force that bears to be reckoned with. A force that can open doors and manipulate with the greatest of deceptors. Satan seeks to destroy and is incredibly patient, resourceful and diligent in his task.

Yes, God is more powerful and wins in the end but the struggles that we fight here on this earth are orchestrated by the same princes and principalities that deceived the greatest of the greats.

There is no gray ground here, no wiggle room and no place to dabble. Our actions bring consequences. They can either be good or bad. A line in the sand drawn yet by the grace of free will the ability to choose where we stand.

Today, choose to stand on the side closest to the One who saves us all. The One who will not falter yet will hold us firm. He will protect us and fight for us.

May we be found worthy of such a Savior.

What doors have you walked through that should have been left alone?

What is the greatest joy today in your life?

What specific action plan can you take today to live worthy?

Words Hurt | 1 Timothy 5:13

Besides, they get into the habit of being idle and going about from house to house. And not only do they become idlers, but also busybodies who talk nonsense, saying things they ought not to.

As we entertain thoughts that are purely for our own enjoyment or perhaps simply to make us feel more secure of whom we are.

"He said this. I heard she said that. Can you believe they did that? She said this about you."

Drawn by sheer curiosity or quite possibly by the morbid desire to be accepted, we tend to listen in places we shouldn't. We tend to talk when it isn't our place to say.

And in the process, lives are destroyed, homes torn apart and lies perpetuated. Friendships become based upon sharing others' lives. In an attempt to build up ourselves, we tear others down.

Or maybe it isn't as severe as that description; after all it's all between friends. Confidences shared then freely distributed between other confidences. No harm no foul. Secrets simply between friends and the lines of friendship can extend quite far in some places.

Yet, what would it look like if we took a step back and only spoke words of truth? Words that are not only filled with good intentions but are also good on their on merit. Words that seek to glorify the King through the praises of His people.

This world is not the promise land and therefore deception and deceit runs deep. Satan will stop at nothing to cause dissension and problems within God's people. And far to often, we are quick to oblige. We see a mirage that is lifted up in our thoughts of what could be if only we say this or that. And when the dust clears, we are left within the ruins.

Choose today to lift up instead of contributing to the noise of deception. Choose to be a person who is known for integrity not deceit, for love and deception, for grace and not condemnation.

Your words. Your choice.

When are you exposed to gossip and unwholesome talk?

What is your response?

What specific action plan can you take today to live worthy?

Not Today Satan | 1 Timothy 5:14

So I counsel younger widows to marry, to have children, to manage their homes and to give the enemy no opportunity for slander.

No opportunity to slander. None at all.

That's the hard part. Each time we step outside of who we should truly be, each time we give in to our worldly desires, even for a moment, the enemy is waiting.

Waiting and watching for us to slip up and he pounces.

It's more than just us. More than just a mistake, more than just ill spoken words, it is ammunition to be used against the Kingdom. God's Kingdom.

We try to live with a clear conscious and strive to do better every day. But if we aren't careful, we begin to compartmentalize our lives. We put God here and our day-to-day activities there. We acknowledge God on Sunday with certain people but we fail to recognize Him through the week, with certain friends or in our homes.

Yet, the enemy watches. He doesn't care where the slip up is made. It doesn't matter if it is hidden where only you can see. He sees, knows and will use it to build a case of to destroy your testimony and if possible your life.

See, Job, gave the enemy nothing. Nothing, yet he was attacked time and time again with permission from the Father. Many times we compare ourselves to Job when trials and consequences come our way even when we have brought them upon ourselves. Even when, we have opened the door to be discredited willingly.

Every day, every moment needs be spent with the full armor of God along with the full submission of our hearts to His will and not ours.

Our words should be used to promote glory not propagate evil. Our actions should be calming and strong not instruments to be used against our very souls.

Live today purposefully aware of each action, each word and each transaction. Did it glorify Him? Are there places and relationships that need space until we are mature enough to use them for His purpose? Where we inadvertently further satan's purpose instead of the Kings.

Live worthy.

Where in your life are you offering a possible weakness in the armor?

What will it take to strengthen it?

What specific action plan can you take today to live worthy?

Evil Exists | 1 Timothy 5:15

Some have in fact already turned away to follow Satan.

And there are that will choose to follow satan. It isn't politically correct to say so and even, in some places, considered to be judgmental to even entertain the thought.

However, it happens.

We envision the darkness of satan to be just that. Darkness. Surrounded by smoke, putrid smells and visual effects of the danger that lurks ahead. And, quite possibly, maybe it does at times really appear this way but it also appears many times as a masquerade of light highlighted by visions of goodness and acceptance. As the masquerade slowly pulls us in, we fall slowly walking towards what we feel is Truth only to awaken to lies entrapped by our own blindness.

Sometimes we know. We really do. We feel the dangers that lurk as soft whispers into our conscious. Our souls bristle as we encounter the evilness that abounds. But quickly we lay such "nonsense" to rest justifying the seemingly goodness that surrounds. Surely someone with success breadth of power and influence is of true goodness. And as we get closer and closer, the facade either falls or entraps us further.

Surprised by the curtain falling exposing the truth, we are genuinely hurt and begin to question everything in our lives. If we have fallen for this, might we also fall for other facades?

Yet, if we were truthful with ourselves we would remember when we were warned and when we stepped over the boundaries into the abyss.

Evil exists, it does. We have to stand ready at all times to stand firm against not only it but sometimes our own worldly desires to follow. We can choose to pretend that it doesn't exist and we lose our greatest protection. Prayer. Praying daily to put on the full armor of God.

Accept that there are those that for whatever reason have chosen to not follow our Christ but to create havoc for other side, to be deceptors, manipulators and instruments of satan. They may not appear to look as the fantasy books and horror portrays them but their intentions are just as deadly.

Don't be caught off-guard. Live each day purposefully aware of the world in which we reside.

Live worthy.

In what areas of your life might you become deceived?

Where have you experienced God's protection in your life?

What specific action plan can you take today to live worthy?

We Are The Church | 1 Timothy 5:16

If any woman who is a believer has widows in her care, she should continue to help them and not let the church be burdened with them, so that the church can help those widows who are really in need.

How many times do we wait for the "church" to do something? Someone needs to reach out to the single parents. Someone needs to contact the widows. Someone should really do something regarding the marriages in our congregation.

Someone.

Someone.

Someone.

However at some point in time, that someone becomes us. We become those who should be the servers instead of the receivers or rather the watchers. We become mentors instead of the mentees. We become the teacher instead of the student.

Yet, we would rather stay the one being guided and coached, the one receiving or the one mentored. We would rather stay as guiders and those who offer constructive criticism instead of stepping in and being the doers. We stay in the familiar role of being rather than doing.

And somewhere along the way, we find that we are the "church". We find that we are the ones responsible. We find that we are refusing to step into the positions that God has laid out for us.

We haven chosen to stay stagnant instead of moving forward.

The church isn't the building nor the pews. And we know this, we do. But do we live this? Do we live exhibiting the same power and magnitude that reflects our King? When God gives us an idea, do we act upon it or do we use it as a responsibility to place upon someone else?

When we stand before Him, and each of us will, we will stand-alone. We will give account of what we have done without excuses upon what the "church" hasn't done. It doesn't take a building, a vote or a committee to be the hands and feet of Christ. The fact that "they" didn't act or that "they" didn't offer will not stand.

Just because the church didn't organize a fellowship doesn't mean we can't invite them to or home. Just because the church hadn't organized a food drive doesn't mean you can't gather the food or that you can't step forward to organize it yourself.

It is time to stop with the excuses, to stop walking in the shadows of deception and to step up and say, "I will obey fully." No excuses. I am the church. I walk with the authority of the King and with that comes the greatest privilege of all. The privilege to serve with no strings or expectations attached.

Live worthy.

What part do you play in the body of the church?

How have you seen Christ at work around you?

What specific action plan can you take today to live worthy?

Honor | 1 Timothy 5:17

The elders who direct the affairs of the church well are worthy of double honor, especially those whose work is preaching and teaching.

It is easy to find fault. It is easy to sit back and watch pointing out the vacancies and the needed areas of improvement.

Those who serve well should receive a double dose of honor.

Yes, there will be those who do not serve well. Unfortunately, there will be those who will take their privileged place of service and use it to further their own personal agendas and those are not the ones who serve well.

But there are also those, who quite possibly serve with their heads humbly bowed with busy hands serving out of the most devotion to Our Father. The ones who are gentle spoken and quick to reach and invest into the lives of those they serve for nothing in return.

The ones who serve well should reserve a double dose of honor.

Unfortunately, we tend to look past these who serve so humbly. We many times fail to recognize the significance of their work that comes from their hands and heart because they always point us towards Him instead of themselves. They offer sacrificial gifts and treasures so numerous that will only be recognized in heaven, as it should be.

But while on this earth, may we treat them with the honor and respect as commanded. May we see past the possible issues and look into their eyes and say, "Thank you." to which they will quickly defer to Christ, as they should because that is their true heart.

In our world where flashiness and loud speech draws our attention, may we look past the worldliness to see realness.

May we identify those in our lives that serve as Christ chose to serve not for our own gain but for those in whom we have been sent. May we take notice of the peacemakers.

Live worthy.

Who do you have in your life that quietly serves?

How do you play the part of the peacemaker in your life?

What specific action plan can you take today to live worthy?

Work | 1 Timothy 5:18

For the Scripture says, "You shall not muzzle an ox when it treads out the grain," and, "The laborer deserves his wages."

After the fall, we were turned out to work, to labor. Labor to survive and labor to bring forth new life.

And, yet, we struggle greatly with it. What is our chosen profession? What should we do? Where should we work?

The world would tell us that prestige and money should be our focus. Stepping-stones should adorn our path as we forge our way into our professional lives. Instead of seeing people for who they are, we see mentors and contacts as we network instead of fellowship.

We divide our lives into our work, our play and sometimes our religion. And they don't intermingle much. It is almost as if we live as if our very lives must have a separation of Church and State.

God created each of us. In each of us is the desire to draw closer to Him. The desire to live in harmony with our Creator. The desire to find what we were created to do and live as such.

The desire to find that moment when you know that this is what you were created for.

Have we felt that? Have we met that moment when we know from our very souls that this is what we were created for? Or are we still living waiting for that day when we "grow up"?

Waiting for that day when we finally get "there" only to find that "there" has moved and "there" we thought would magically complete us doesn't fulfill us. Instead, we see another "there" in the distant horizon.

How much time do we waste trying to fulfill the world's expectations of ourselves instead of only focusing on Christ's? We can't have it all as much as the world will seduce us into believing.

We can't. We can be lured into believing we can but we eventually realize that to seek something else is to not seek Him. His way, His purpose, His direction. It is one way only.

Seek Him. Find what you were created to do and do it. It doesn't mean that life will fall into place and all will be easy. But it does mean that your very soul will seem at rest. You will find freedom that isn't contingent on circumstances. You will find the ever-elusive "it" that isn't bound by the margins of this world.

Live worthy.

What are you continually trying to attain that remains just beyond your reach?

What times in your life have you felt as if you are doing what you were to do?

What specific action plan can you take today to live worthy?

Do Not Entertain | 1 Timothy 5:19

Do not entertain an accusation against an elder unless it is brought by two or three witnesses.

Do not even entertain. Don't mull it over. Don't think about it. Don't even listen to it unless it is confirmed by two or more.

Think about how our social circles would change if we extended this to all accusations and gossip that we hear throughout our day. Instead, we tend to listen putting into our mind the possibility of poisonous words and accusations that seemingly take on a life of themselves as soon as we listen. Even false, they taint our view and bring doubt into our mind.

Do not entertain.

But it is ever so easy to do so. To listen is to be a good friend, a supporter or a sounding board. However, sometimes to listen is to be the medium satan uses to weave his very lies to twist and to develop a plausible story line that can bring even the strongest to their knees.

To listen is to be on the ready to preserve Truth and the church. However too many times once the lies take on a life of their own, the Truth isn't the moderator anymore. The standard has already been compromised and we have been the catalyst.

Each day brings promises anew and each day brings attacks that satan designs. Each day. We must stand ready. Aware of what we listen to. Aware of whom we condemn.

Wise beyond ourselves leaning into His wisdom and direction.

The more we find ourselves aligned with Christ the more our sensitivity to evil will abound. To be surrounded in evil every moment of every day, slowly desensitizes ourselves to it and we begin to accept a new normal. We must be careful that daily we are protected by His armor. Not our strength but His.

And in His strength, we will find the strength not to listen. In His strength, we will lose the desire to be a part of "the know". In His strength, we will make a difference.

Live worthy. Live different.

Where are you surrounded by gossip and negative speech?

How can you change the dialogue?

What specific action plan can you take today to live worthy?

First Stone Thrown | 1 Timothy 5:20

Those who sin are to be rebuked publicly, so that the others may take warning.

And this is the one we seem to have no difficulty doing. Of course, it pains us greatly and we do it all in "Christian love" but it is one that we seemingly can do wholeheartedly quite easily Christians and non-believers alike.

Make an example of those who have strayed. Bring other's sin out into the open. Share publicly so others might learn. Or maybe we just randomly throw out other's sins just because we can.

But, just because we can doesn't mean we should.

Many times those who throw the first stones are the ones who throw for their own needs. They throw so they might not be discovered in their own pile of muck. They throw to look important to anyone watching. They throw because others throw. They throw because satan's lies abound so they throw with all the hatred and self-righteousness that they can muster.

And at the end of the day, all hope is seemingly lost for redemption and restoration. And the self-righteous quickly turn to this verse, saying that they were only carrying out their duty as they were commanded.

And it hurts them as much as it hurts the sinner in question.

The prostitute knows where her lot is in life. She knows all too well. She doesn't have to be reminded.

The adulterous spouse understands their wrong path without the scorning eyes and words. The thief, the gossiper and the list goes on and on. They know. They live with their condemnation, with their choices that have led to a path of destruction.

Instead of constantly being reminded of their sin, perhaps we should remind them of their value, their being the creation of a Creator that makes no mistakes. Remind them of love, not enablement, but love with no agenda.

Use Godly wisdom, that most often than not calls us to walk along beside with arms around instead of in front with fingers pointing. There is a time for public correction but His place, His Words, His timing. When we take ourselves, our pride and our emotions out of the equation, we open the moment for God to truly work.

Always.

Love first. Live worthy.

Where have you placed blame and judgment that wasn't yours to place?

Who can you reach out to and just love?

What specific action plan can you take today to live worthy?

Treated Different | 1 Timothy 5:21

I charge you, in the sight of God and Christ Jesus and the elect angels, to keep these instructions without partiality, and to do nothing out of favoritism.

And this is perhaps one of the most difficult of all. Without partiality.

In a world in which contacts and networking is of great priority, there is a common belief perhaps to all that there is favoritism. Some people tend to be treated better than others as a simple result of whom they know, where they live and how they look.

They are treated different.

They receive always the benefit of the doubt. They receive favor and encounter open arms and warm smiles. They are destined to succeed, or so it seems, so everyone seems to align themselves with that same line of thought. Born into unearned favor, they receive simply because they are.

And then, there are those who are on the opposite side of the spectrum. Those upon whom smiles are nonexistent and favor is never on their side. By the simple demeanor of those of whom they encounter, they quickly summarize their lot in life. A lot that is considered less than. A lot that is surrounded by scrutiny and implied deception. A lot that fosters ill will even when none is encountered.

Treated different simply because of whom the world is identifies on as such.

Treated different.

Treated so differently that it is almost impossible to believe that in God's eye we are all equal. No one favorite. Equality in its purest form. Equality so pure that we can't imagine. The ultimate level playing ground in which we all find ourselves upon. Sure, we create a facade that demonstrates various levels of inequality.

Levels that raise others up towards the heavens while some are lower than the ground on which we walk. But those levels mean nothing just smoke screen that man has bought into. Lies that satan has woven to keep us from understanding that we are all loved greatly. We are all created by the Great I Am.

Each one of us.

Today, look at those who surround as who they truly are. They are creations of God Almighty. Each and every one.

Live worthy.

Are there times when you feel less than?

Can you say, "God loves me" and truly believe it? How can you foster this to yourself and others?

What specific action plan can you take today to live worthy?

Not With Haste | 1 Timothy 5:22

Do not be hasty in the laying on of hands, and do not share in the sins of others. Keep yourself pure.

We want to help. We do.
We want to reach at and grab hold, fix and clean up. We want to make it better.

But sometimes, it isn't ours to fix.

Daily we are inundated with people in our lives who need something. Sometimes there are physical needs. Sometimes spiritual needs and, sometimes, the needs are emotional. Some of the needs come from those who are nameless in our world and other times they are from our most intimate.

And all too often, we are quick to reach out.

Isn't that what we have been instructed to do? We look to the Great Samaritan as an example and we strive to help the least of these. But what if our help actually causes destruction? What if our help stands in the way of actual help? What if our help pulls them away from seeking God and instead points, unknowingly, towards a materialistic or temporary world.

What if in our frenzy to help we hurt instead?

Discernment in all things. All things. While our knee-jerk reaction may appear at first to be the most compassionate act known to mankind, we must be intentional to follow our Father's lead. Always.

While it might seem as if a house, a car, food or money would solve problems, sometimes it points them towards us instead of towards Him. Sometimes, it leads away from the very purpose as to why.

For His Glory. Period.

In this battle for souls, sometimes we lose perspective. We reach out to fix this temporary home instead of enduring.

There are times when material things provide the vehicle to present the gospel. However, there are other times when God asks us to go deeper, look past the material world and invest fully in relationships. There are times when our undivided attention, time and the sharing of our life are what are required. Sharing of ourselves with arms outstretched.

And, perhaps most difficult, there are times when we are directed to stand down. To wait. Instructed not to act now but rather continue our walk of obedience without ever engaging. "But, we could fix this easily," our very hearts cry out. Perhaps. However without obedience to our Father's command, we will find ourselves walking in our own strength and at the end of the day wondering what went wrong. Wondering why it didn't work even with our best intentions. Wondering why things are actually worse than when we started.

And it is at that moment that we turn to God. Finally, we ask for direction.

We will make mistakes. We will. And tomorrow, we will be wiser to them. The key is to not become jaded but to become intentionally His.

Not His out of desperation when we are at the bottom of the barrel but rather be as close to Him during our times of greatest joy as we are during times that we are most lost.

Live intentional. Live worthy.

What propels you to help others?

How are you sure it is His will for you to help and not your own?

What specific action plan can you take today to live worthy?

Trust The Process | 1 Timothy 5:23

Stop drinking only water, and use a little wine because of your stomach and your frequent illnesses.

A personal letter from Paul to Timothy that contains personal direction regarding Timothy's health. This reminds us of the humanness of our authors. They weren't superheroes. They weren't God-like themselves. They were men just like ourselves today who had stomach issues just like us today amongst other things.

They lived surrounded by a world that didn't understand. A world filled with sin and chaos. A world that instead of collectively searching for Truth was seeking pleasure through the pursuit of all things pleasurable. All things.

Yet, they chose to live set apart. They chose to live different. They chose another way. A most unpopular way was chosen to live their lives. Lives that they lived out of obedience. Humble obedience.

When Christ was betrayed and arrested in an olive grove near the valley of Kidron, Peter tried to defend Him by cutting of the ear of one of the soldiers, Jesus quickly healed his ear while instructing Peter to put His sword away.

At times it is tempting to take things in our own hands. Just as Peter, to pull out our swords whether they be literally or figuratively. We want to be like Peter to stop the unfolding of events that are outside of our realm. We want to restore what we would consider true justice.

However, sometimes we must trust the outcome even when the process seems intolerable. God has this.

Just as Christ knew what ultimately awaited Him once the soldiers would take Him into custody. He saw past the unfair trials, verbal slander, vicious whippings and ultimately crucifixion and saw the redemption for mankind.

A sight so far removed from the immediate human emotion at that time that Peter wouldn't have been able to even conceive the possibility that any good would be able to come out of his immediate circumstances just as sometimes we can't see past the immediate hurt, anger and betrayal.

We are called to stand and to stand firm. But we are called to stand Christ-like. He built relationships based upon love. He came to this world not to condemn it but to redeem it. He taught his disciples the same. We can love and serve anywhere sharing the Truth by actions, embraces and a testimony of a life lived, not out of judgment, but out of love.

And while there are times quite possibly when controlled and humbled anger is called for as Jesus demonstrated while clearing out the temple, those times are few and far between. Jesus rarely used anger and rebuked his disciples when they tried. He also saw through the agendas of those who tended to speak "Truth" loudly with condemnation. We must be wise. Always. Now if ever, it is most important to live as Jesus would live and to react as He would react.

Yes, we stand firm, but perhaps most importantly we stand Christ-like.

Live worthy.

What does it look like in your life to stand Christ-like?

What role does anger play in your life?

What specific action plan can you take today to live worthy?

Deeper Than Skin | 1 Timothy 5:24

The sins of some men are obvious, reaching the place of judgment ahead of them; the sins of others trail behind them.

Those are the easy ones, yes? The ones that we can observe, quickly assess and identify the sins that encompass their lives. Consequences of actions and judgments occur right out in the open spotlighting a life mired in bad choices and decisions. The lies, the anger, betrayal, the pride and arrogance give way to destruction as relationships and joy seem to fade away.

And then there are the subtle ones.

The ones whose lives look shiny on the outside. Well-put together and lived in a manner that blends well into society. Rules and relationships followed in a manner that doesn't distract nor draw attention to a life that really is not as it is. A life that may masquerade in the inner circle, contributing to the building of a Kingdom until gifting the ultimate kiss of betrayal.

Those are the ones that catch us by surprise. The ones in whom we have confidence in not only their ability but in their seemingly spiritual journey. The ones that we have garnered advice and support from not realizing that their counsel was from own agendas and not from the guidance of the Fathers. Sometimes, the cracks show. There are little glitches here and there. We see quite possibly a lot of work and not so much fruit. We see a lot of doers yet not a lot of believers.

In the trash dump, garbage is picked through to glean anything of worth albeit glass, plastic, cardboard, food and metal. The trash pile is then set on fire to burn away the outward waste to reveal the possibility of valuables underneath. Sometimes, the fire gives way to precious and valuable metals. Sometimes, it gives way to simply ashes of burned trash.

When we look at lives, when we look at our own, we must look deeper than the skin. We must look deeper than what the world would have us see. What is there once the fire burns? Is there precious metal or ashes that scatter with the wind?

Live worthy.

What would be left of your life if the "fire" were to burn away what is observed by the human eye?

How can precious metal be created instead of ashes in the wind?

What specific action plan can you take today to live worthy?

Listen Closely | 1 Timothy 5:25

In the same way, good deeds are obvious, and even those that are not cannot be hidden.

Public opinion. The need to garner support and encouragement from "those that be".

We live in a world that reaches, searches for approval and for acceptance from others. Given the wide variety of those in the world, we can typically garner a gathering of supportive people in almost any endeavor if we seek in just the right places. We can find that mountaintop and shout, "Look at me and what I've done" and they will look and praise regardless of what we might be doing.

Or, we can surround ourselves with people who are naysayers and constantly pick and prod slowly tearing us apart while reaching deeper and deeper into our lives. They, under the guise of mentorship and love, critique and badger until we succumb our very thoughts to themselves. Maybe they are right, maybe we aren't good enough, smart enough, and the list goes on and on until we soon become a skeleton of ourselves.

Satan works an interesting game. Pride and the need for love and acceptance constantly grates against our desire to live in humility and unconditional love. He constantly pokes and adjusts while prowling to cause dissension and division to cause pain and hurt.

And then there are those who walk quietly even though their footsteps leave a wake of goodness in their path.

They walk close to the Father so that any good deed is a reflection of Him, not them. So close, that any arrow of lies, anger or betrayal from this world is quickly reflected by His armor. Public opinion is merely two words as they set their eyes on things with eternal value.

The type of people that the rest of us seek to bask in the air of their calmness and joy. We see a little piece of heaven as we witness their walk.

We can choose who we wish to follow. We will always be measured and judged by the world, but the real battle is in the decision upon whom to listen. Do we listen to those who will encourage us blindly, those who ridicule us for their own good or He who holds us in the palm of His Hand?

Choose wisely. Live worthy.

Who impacts your life?

How do you know that they guide you from a Godly place?

What specific action plan can you take today to live worthy?

Living Testimony | 1 Timothy 6:1

All who are under the yoke of slavery should consider their masters worthy of full respect, so that God's name and our teaching may not be slandered.

It is way bigger than us. Way bigger.

The waves that traverse out upon each action that we make throughout our day speak volumes to those who are watching and seeking. We misinterpret our smallness with insignificance. We mistake that our actions, our lives are just one of many or that our days are just one of many that in the grand scheme of the world doesn't really matter.

There's always a second chance, yes?

And for us, maybe there is but what of those that are watching us? What about the seekers and doubters? What do they see when we act out? We will falter. We will make mistakes. We are still sinners and not perfect yet covered by His grace. But what about the times when we act out purposefully and intentional knowing full well we are outside of His will. The long line in the grocery store. The teenager who bullies our own children. The co-worker who lies. The moments of freedom that we have when no one seems to be looking. The frustration in traffic, in family, in life. Our "personal" worlds.

How do we respond? That's what is important. Not our situation, not the outcome but our response within the storm. Do we grab hold of the oars and stand firm or do we yell at the captain and crew?

Do we marvel at its intensity or do we cower in self-defense? Do we stand always in testimony of our Father?

Always.

This misinterpretation then must be carefully measured against the opposite end of the spectrum in pride and arrogance.

There are times when we stand and stand firm unwavering and then we notice that we are standing and like Peter, we look away from Christ.

And we falter. We sink. Maybe we don't physically fall but we fall in our character. We forget where our strength came from and we begin to boast and judge and, truthfully, cause more damage than if we might have just fallen.

There are no days off from being a child of God. None. Satan will tell is that it is okay to let our guard down, to live a little. We deserve it. Satan also lies. Each moment of each day is a moment that we can't take back, can't relive. Moments constantly being walked on the balance between the heavens and evilness of this world.

May we forever life as a living testimony.

Live worthy.

What does your daily testimony reveal to others about the King?

Where in your life do you tend to lose control? How can you alleviate this?

What specific action plan can you take today to live worthy?

Teach And Urge On | 1 Timothy 6:2

Those who have believing masters are not to show less respect for them because they are brothers. Instead, they are to serve them even better, because those who benefit from their service are believers, and dear to them. These are the things you are to teach and urge on them.

We spend many of our days trying to stay politically correct. We might subtly suggest but how often do we urge on? How often to ask those around us, those close to us about their walk with Christ? Furthermore, urging them on to fight the good fight.

Do we simply not have time?

Are we too tired to get involved once our day-to-day life is lived?

Are we afraid to step on toes?

So we pray for them or at least we commit to pray for them. Our intentions are good, however our follow-through oftentimes gets lost in life. We forget until we see them again and then we remember. Only to commit again with no follow-through.

It's hard. Well, it's not really hard like physical labor hard or emotionally hard it is just hard to fit it all in. Our intentions are good but our urging on tends to fall short until it seems to merely be a passing thought.

And, yet, our adversary urges continuously in our lives. He urges us to believe his lies, to falter and to fail. He urges us through fear of loss, danger and uncertainty.

He urges us prancing around things within our reach if only we will succumb. He urges us to seek the pleasure of this world and forfeit the discipline of righteousness. He urges us to taste the pasture on the other side and leave our own homes promising greener grass just on the other side.

He doesn't let up. He doesn't stop. He lies continuously.

And, yet, we can't seem to find the time to battle, as he should be battled. We need to encourage our brothers and sisters urging them to be strong and stay close to the Father. Constantly evaluating what really is important in our lives and investing there first and letting the materialness of this world have the leftovers. Too many times, those that God has given us get to scraps and things that will not stand the test of eternity get our very best.

Choose differently. Yes, it will be a radical change but it will change lives forever.

Who has God given you to love, cherish and guide?

How can you assure that they don't get the leftovers of your energy, time and attention?

What specific action plan can you take today to live worthy?

Pride | 1 Timothy 6:3-4

If anyone teaches otherwise and does not agree to the sound instruction of our Lord Jesus Christ and to godly teaching, they are conceited and understand nothing.

Pride will make us fall every time.

It starts out small, as most falls do, a little step here, a small change there and a little blurring of the teaching in the middle. It starts out, quite possibly, with even the best of intentions. This is what is takes to bring them in, to help them accept so they will listen.

So, we alter the Truth just a bit. Just enough so that it is palatable for those around us. Not quite as radical, not quite as bold, perhaps a "softer version" of it all.

And it works.

Or so it seems. Our classes increase in numbers, our friends will listen and converse and those we've had trouble reaching for years have suddenly begun to take note of our new twist on our faith. They recognize the newer version as being more forgiving and loving. They respond which encourages us even further.

We've found a new way.

A new way into deception. A new way paved and encouraged by satan, himself. By adding to, taking away and twisting as we deem needed, we have stopped taking the Truth to the nations and instead are taking our own flavor that holds no merit at all.

The Truth is the Truth. No deviations.

For those on the outside looking in, we wonder if these teachers have ever really known the Truth at all. Do they fear Him at all? Do they understand the ramifications of their deviations in teaching His Word?

It seems as if there is a short distinction between total obedience and complete deception.

We must constantly be on guard with ourselves making sure that the Truth in which we share with others is the real deal.

Yes, they might listen further if we water it down a bit or twist a few notions around but the moment we add to or take away from the Truth make it no longer Truth but merely man made words. Words that will not withstand the test of eternity.

Pray for those who have been so deceived. Pray for an awakening. Speak boldly when you share God's Word. He will soften hearts. It is our job to just follow in obedience and share.

Live worthy.

When have you been tempted to adjust the Gospel so that it was easier to present?

Who have you shared the Gospel to within the last couple of days? Weeks? Months?

What specific action plan can you take today to live worthy?

Unhealthy Interest | 1 Timothy 6:4-5

They have an unhealthy interest in controversies and quarrels about words that result in envy, strive, malicious talk, evil suspicions and constant friction between men of corrupt mind, who have been robbed of the Truth and who think that godliness is a means to financial gain.

How different would our lives be if we simply refused to engage in controversies? How many negative thoughts and ideas do we willingly bring into our world as we listen to malicious talk and evil suspicions? How often do we entertain those whose minds are corrupt filled with envy and strive?

And we wonder why our lives are filled with constant friction?

There are those in this world who will attempt to extinguish the joy in our lives. Perhaps not purposefully, perhaps even just pawns themselves, they seek to surround our lives with utter chaos. Their words are dripping of gossip, lies and envious words. As soon as they hear, they can't wait to spread.

And, we willingly choose to listen.

We control who and what we bring into our lives. Sometimes, we get caught up into the busyness of the world and we find ourselves seemingly as a ship at sea trying to just stay afloat. We try not to create any more waves and just try to sail. Yet, we were the ones who, purposefully or not, have placed our ship amongst dark waters. And as the words continue to fill our life out of these relationships, we become more and more entangled.

Likewise, there are those who find game out of arguing. They find sport out of trying to "trip" us up and trying to find our weak spots in our faith and pointing them out quickly. They hold court and judgment based upon a few words here and there. Never truthfully seeking for themselves, they are merely trying to "enlighten" those around them.

God has made us wise. He has filled us with great wisdom. Great wisdom. We must be intentional about whom we choose to listen. We must become disciplined against listening to gossip and malicious talk. Purposefully walking away, disengaging and protecting ourselves and our families from the chaos that seeks to enter.

We can do that. Really.

And by doing so, not only do we stop the unhealthy conversation from entering our minds, but quite possibly we may cause them to pause and ponder why we no longer engage. Why we no longer listen? And, perhaps someday they will ask why? The question that opens the door to share the greatest Story ever told.

We are called to live different from this world. In it, not of it.

Do we?

Live worthy.

How do you live different from this world?

How do you respond when someone questions your faith?

What specific action plan can you take today to live worthy?

Contentment | 1 Timothy 6:6

But Godliness with contentment is great gain.

The ever-elusive key to personal fulfillment or so it seems and then to add Godly on top of that and we find ourselves searching for another way, another door, and another path.

Surely, our flesh cries, there is another way. We strive to find contentment in who we are, in our status and position in this world. We insist on finding contentment in our family being careful to try to orchestrate that perfect Norman Rockwell moments. We search for contentment in all things looking for that place to be.

Yet, our soul never rests.

Created to fulfill a specific purpose with the desires to be in tune with our Creator, true contentment will only be found in that place.

Yet, the world will push against us. The closer that we seemingly get to that moment the more chaos and despair the world will throw our way. Almost as if to say, "There is a better way. Come and wallow in your despair. Cry out foul. Retreat. Retreat. Retreat."

But the decaying world is what has brought us to this place and will not stand the test of eternity. Lies. Lies that offer the "world" in a silver platter which are lies that fade quickly in the wind. Lies that offer comfort and acceptance yet that will fail to fulfill.

Lies that offer prestige and honor that are based on shaky ground. Lies that when the curtain falls reveal that contentment was never part of the plan.

Contentment dwells in knowing Him. Found only in His presence, it can never be taken nor marred but rather it can be cultivated and grown. It comes not from flashy plans and schemes but rather from daily walking close to Him and finding one's value greater than this world.

Contentment is in resting assuredly that He holds all of our tomorrow's whether on this earth or in heaven.

Contentment here doesn't come easy. Sometimes it is found in the steadfast refusal to experience anything else. The world would call on us to respond from a worldly perspective in anger and grief, yet, He is the only One to deliver us from it all.

Where does our contentment lie? With whom do we fall to when our reality suddenly shifts? In whose camp do we seek who we truly are? Do our lives reveal the proof in our answers? Do we live as ones who seek our contentment only from Him?

Where do you find the most contentment? Where does your soul find rest?

How do you reflect joy that can only come from Him?

What specific action plan can you take today to live worthy?

Psalm 139 | 1 Timothy 6:7

For we brought nothing into this world, and we can take nothing out of it.

The ultimate equalizer, yes?

When we all face our last breath on this earth, and we each will someday, we will transition from it holding nothing.

Nothing.

Oh, we may be buried with our favorite keepsakes and charms. But they, as our earthly body also, will stay part of this earth and we will stand before the King.

We spend much of our lives amassing things. Possessions. Some big and some small. Some valuable and others only to the eye of the beholder. Some we hold tight and others we simply store. Perhaps, the storehouse is filled with money while some fill it with people. Yet, sometimes it is just the title of who we are and what we do.

We rest in the security of knowing that they are ours. It is who we are in the world.

But have we built for ourselves our own individual Towers of Babel?

I did this and I did that. I am this and I am that. This is my creation from within this world.

When we stand before the throne, there will be no smoke screen.

There will be a clarity that has exceeded all clarity. We will know, that deep in your soul know.

We will finally see as our earthly trimmings fade away what really has eternal value and what was simply just toiling in sun.

We will leave this world as we came into it. There won't be a line of us waiting in First Class with our Prada luggage nor will there be a line of us with all of our possessions in a ripped plastic bag.

There won't be those of us with concierges nor those of us who are slaves. The identifying factor will be on where we placed our trust, our faith, our hope.

We can believe that our "Towers of Babel" will never fall but that they will grow and grow and grow. We can surround ourselves with people, money and things clenching them tight in our hands.

But, we will lose.

We all have an appointed time. Psalm 139. He knows our days before we have lived one. He knows.

So as we walk through today, let's reflect on what we subconsciously have mentally and emotionally packed to take with us and then see how we can use it to further Kingdom work instead more personal gain.

Live worthy.

What is your "tower of Babel? What material things have you collected and treasure above all things?

How can you invest more fully upon His work instead of the world's?

What specific action plan can you take today to live worthy?

Content | 1 Timothy 6:8

But if we have food and clothing, we will be content with that.

Content defined as being in a state of peaceful happiness.

What does it take to make us content? Wait, not just content but to be in a state of peaceful happiness?

That new car that we don't have? The perfect husband or wife we are searching for? The child we have yet to hold in our arms? The ones we've lost to be back? Health to be restored? Money in the bank? The next position at work? The house remodeled, the house cleaned, the jewelry we've been watching to go on sale.

Somehow, someway we've turned contentment into gaining what we don't have at this moment but hope to have in the future. Our state of peaceful happiness is not in this moment but in the future. It is ever elusive.

So we work and strive to reach a state of happiness that we will never achieve because that is not where contentment will be found. Our expectations, our bar of happiness has been tainted by the evil of this world. Lies have woven and Truths have been covered revealing a life that is dependent on what we have obtained not in Whose we are.

Statistics demonstrate that we are amongst the richest people in the world. Those of us who have cars, homes and money at our disposal are living lives that have been goldenly blessed. We have found favor.

Yet, many times we believe that we are amongst the poor, that we have so very little while there is so very much that we can acquire. If we only had more.

We throw ourselves into our jobs not for the sake of fulfilling our God-given calling but rather to receive payment in order to fill our lives with what will make us happy. We forego opportunities to invest in the people God has sent to us in order to build relationships and instead use our time to make more money, pay those bills and be happy.

But we aren't happy?

We look forward to retirement so we can be happy but we don't find it there either. Perhaps, just perhaps our definition of contentment, of finding that place of peaceful happiness has become distorted. Perhaps, it is time to take back our true selves and live no longer in the bondage that satan has created. No more.

Today, we will find peaceful happiness. For we will look in our closet and we will see clothes. We will look in our refrigerators and on our shelves find food and this will be our new marker that determines our contentment.

Not money, not wealth, not friends nor the size of our house, job or body but simply in the assurance that He will clothe us and feed us. It's not going to be easy. It's a mindset. A choice. Do we believe Him or do we believe the world? Once we make the choice, we have to develop the discipline to back it up. When the thought of discontent comes into our mind, we have to toss them out. Look at the clothes on our bodies and the fullness of our bellies and find contentment there.

Some of us have been blessed far greater than food and clothes. In fact, I dare say that each one of us reading this has ample clothing and food and the rest is simply the cherry on the top.

Choose to evaluate your life differently today. It isn't about comparing what we have to the rest of the world and to find contentment in what we have through being guilted. It is about being obedient to our Father who says to find peaceful happiness in the provision of clothing and food.

Evaluate your life today? Are you clothed? Have you eaten? Do you have a job? Do you have a house? Do you have a car? Do you have above a third grade education?

Welcome to peaceful happiness.

Live worthy.

List your material possessions.

How does it feel to live as one of the wealthiest in the world?

What specific action plan can you take today to live worthy?

Pick Wisely | 1 Timothy 6:9

Those who want to get rich fall into temptation and a trap and into many foolish and harmful desires that plunge people into ruin and destruction.

It's all about the motive.

There are those who are able to work and amass riches and use their gains for the furthering of God's Kingdom. However, the majority falls into the trappings of this world and lose all sight of healthy bearings.

The pursuit of riches has lost many in its wake. Family, friends, health and spiritual growth are all set-aside for just a moment so that the work can be done. We explain to ourselves that it is only for this moment because tomorrow or at least some point in the near future we will have all that we need to have.

And then we can focus on the things really important to us.

We realize what is truly important. We do. We know that God should come first followed by our family. We know and desire that our homes are filled with peaceful family atmospheres and that we connect on intimate levels with those we love.

We just need to do this first.

We know that our marriages are important and take time to nurture. We understand the argument of quality versus quantity.

We know.

It's just, well, this is what we have to do now and later we can do what we know we should do.

But later rarely, if ever, comes. We continue to buy into the "American dream".

A dream that was once focused on families achieving together yet has somehow morphed into individualism at such an incredible rate that competitions exist within our own homes between husbands and wives. We continue to fall into the trappings that satan spins.

Glorious trappings, of course. A nicer house, nicer car, nicer this and nicer that. A bigger title, another promotion, bonus and corner office. More money, more money and the potential for more money.

And he will "bless" these endeavors as much as he is allowed for each time we taste success we are rewarded for following a path that takes us farther and farther from our true purpose in the world. And as we begin to lose those most important to us, he continues to weave lies assuring us that it isn't our fault and we are not to blame. We are just not understood and appreciated for all that we sacrifice.

Because it is a sacrifice isn't it?

Perhaps, though, the sacrifice is of our true purpose in our lives. Perhaps it is at the sacrifice of never finding that true calling that God placed on our lives. Perhaps, the sacrifice is found in the loss of all that our Father has blessed us with.

We can argue all we want and cry foul but the Truth is the Truth. It just is. Argue. Take a stand. Draw the line in the sand.

Just realize to whom you are aligning with when you purposefully choose to take a stand against God. There are only two choices in this world. Only two.

Pick wisely. Live worthy.

How many hours do you work a week?

How many hours do you spend focused on your family and those He has given you?

What specific action plan can you take today to live worthy?

Empty Riches | 1 Timothy 6:10

For the love of money is a root of all kinds of evil. Some people, eager for money, have wandered from the faith and pierced themselves with many griefs.

Money and the quest to amass more.

The lies associated with money are simple really. Its web of deceit closely mimics that longing deep in our soul for our Creator. It brings promises of security, love, happiness, the fulfillment of all of our desires, and the list goes and on.

Empty promises.

Assurances that all will be well, that we can make our own way, that we are in control.

Empty assurances.

Empty promises and assurances that bring with it destruction in their way. As we delve deeper and deeper, we find that it isn't really us that is amassing money but rather money that is amassing us. Initially, the sacrifices are small. A late night here or there, a holiday, an additional project, an additional job, short cut here and short cut there.

At first it may seem easy or maybe even a little difficult. Just enough either way that pride begins to take root. We can finally have everything we ever wanted bought and paid for by our own hand. Me, myself and I. And as our wealth builds and the tables begin to turn, we see glimpses of our own mortality.

Glimpses that don't fit into the world we have created.

And this perhaps is where satan attempts to seal the deal. He weaves more lies about death and what lies beyond. He takes our childhood faith and attempts to poke holes in it. He takes our greediness and fear of insignificance and uses it to battle for our souls and too often, he wins.

Its not that we can't have riches and inherit the Kingdom of God, we can.

However, there is a very fine line between having and worshipping. A line that many of us fail to toe successfully and during the balance, we lose everything.

We must live cautiously always on the battlefield. We must be wise and purposeful ready to lay aside anything that may have the potential to draw that fatal cut. We must walk close enough with Him that anything not from Him riles our soul and we quickly flee. Satan masquerades in the opulent and shiny of this world and he offers it to us at the deferred price of our soul.

Choose wisely. Live different.

What entices you from Him?

How can you assure that you are not "toeing the line" too closely?

What specific action plan can you take today to live worthy?

Flee. Pursue | 1 Timothy 6:11

But you, man of God, flee from all of this, and pursue righteousness, godliness, faith, love, endurance and gentleness.

Flee. Pursue.

Not passive words but descriptive verbs requiring action on our part. Instructions given to offer us direction. Guidance imparted to us to give permission to literally flee from the evilness and temptations of this world.

Too often, though, we try to endure both sides. We listen to instructions we should never hear, we entertain circles we should never enter into and we remain long after the darkness has been brought to light. We want to be liked. We want to help. We want to make a difference. And when we stay when we should have run, when we linger when we should have walked or when we dabble when we should have left, we wait passively for God to save us.

When all along we could have just walked away. We should have been obedient and simply have fled right from the beginning.

If we flee from the beginning, we skip all of the baggage that we slowly tend to collect. If we run instead of linger, we forego the pain and suffering that will be heaped upon us. If we leave instead of dabble, we allow ourselves to be protected instead of willingly walking into the gallows.

Live Worthy

We, alone, control what we allow ourselves, our minds and souls be privy to as we live in this world. A choice. Initially, fleeing is difficult. It follows both from the outside and from inside of our own mind. People who are used to us partaking in gossip, greed and earthly desires will expect us to continue as we have in the past.

First by lightheartedly pushing then by hurtful slurs and threats. We will lose relationships. We will live set apart. Invitations will cease and conversations change.

Perhaps though, the greatest battleground is in our mind. We play through old memories, broken promises and unfiltered dreams. We linger at what could have been choosing to entertain our emotions from within our mind. We harbor regrets and anger. We think thoughts that we would never speak for fear that someone might hear. They stay unfettered in the recesses of our mind.

Flee. No questions or arguments. Flee.

Pursue love, righteousness, godliness, faith, endurance and gentleness instead. Again, active engagement, active choices. Each of us chooses how we desire to live. Do we flee the things of this world and pursue those of our Creature?

Choose wisely. Live worthy.

What is your response when negative thoughts enter your mind?

How can you adjust this?

What specific action plan can you take today to live worthy?

Fight The Good Fight | 1 Timothy 6:12

Fight the good fight of the faith. Take hold of the eternal life to which you were called when you made your good confession in the presence of many witnesses.

The eternal life to which we were called.

This is what we are to take hold of as we fight the good fight of the faith. This is what will propel us forward, will encourage us and guide us. It will sustain us through this world giving hope when there appears to be none. Offering peace when our bodies can't comprehend the trauma, it will feed our soul as if manna from the sky.

If only we would allow it to bathe us freely.

Instead, we allow fear to seep in. We struggle to find intellectually sound arguments and theories that allow us to seemingly remain in control. We focus on what we can build and formulate with our hands and minds. We find peace in bank accounts and people. We find security in who the world says we are.

Until we don't.

The world will only allow us to pretend to conquer it so far. The master of deception allows us to be lulled into thinking we are the masters of our universe until we begin to flex our own muscles and thoughts, until we try to break away and then it willingly allows us to see the casualties that have fallen in our wake. At that moment, the tables turn and guilt is heaped upon our head.

Or perhaps, we never try to break away or stand apart but rather embrace all this world has to offer. We eagerly anticipate each stage mapped out in our life. From being single to married to family to empty nesters to senior citizens, we see the map laid out.

Until it's not.

Then we fight the good fight for our life. We turn to every medical advancement and possibility.

We cling to statistics that offer slivers of hope. We seek wisdom and direction from those who have devoted their lives to keeping others alive. We place our security in them, the machines and results.

And sometimes it seems to work; yet sometimes it doesn't.

What would our lives look like if the greatest fight that we have ever fought were the good fight of the faith? What if the greatest anger that we have ever experienced was due to a slight upon our faith? When we compare the moments in our lives that we have fought the fight, does our faith even play a part? We fight for love. We fight for honor. We fight for possession. We fight to be first in line or to win the best bargain. But do we ever fight the good fight for our faith? I dare say, do we even remember what it would look like?

It would revolutionize our lives if every decision, every relationship, every dollar spent was made in the light of eternity.

Live different.

What is the good fight that you are currently fighting?

How would your life change if the "good fight" was focused on the Kingdom?

What specific action plan can you take today to live worthy?

The Good Confession | 1 Timothy 6:13-16

In the sight of God, who gives life to everything, and of Christ Jesus, who while testifying before Pontius Pilate made the good confession, I charge you to keep this command without spot or blame until the appearing of our Lord Jesus Christ, which God will bring about in his own time—God, the blessed and only Ruler, the King of kings and Lord of lords, who alone is immortal and who lives in unapproachable light, whom no one has seen or can see. To him be honor and might forever. Amen.

In front of a judge who would seemingly decide His worldly fate, He made the good confession when it might have been so much easier to take a different path. He made the good confession. Pilate asked a direct question and Jesus answered with clarity and boldness. He answered with humility instead of arrogance.

How many times have we been given the opportunity to make "the good confession" and we have simply taken the different path? Perhaps it just didn't seem to be the right time, we didn't seem to have just the right relationship or we just didn't want to get involved so we don't. Or perhaps our response depends on where we are at when asked? Perhaps when we are in a place where an explanation of our faith will be appreciated or even heralded, we speak of our allegiance loudly. However, when we find ourselves in places where our faith will attract attention or quite possibly require, at the very least, an explanation, we quietly refrain from answering directly or perhaps not even at all.

Yet when we find ourselves needing Him and His provisions, we speak loudly. When we found ourselves wronged or treated unjustly by this world, we run quickly to His shelter. When we find ourselves knocking at death's door, we call out His name and He answers us. Every single time.

He reaches and draws us to Him without rebuke but rather with the softness of a Father who simply knows. He loves us. He just does. He gave us life and provides us with a Light that darkness can't extinguish. No matter how dark.

A Light that shines through our darkest night and rivals our darkest day. It never fades nor does it ever cease to exist. A Light that isn't determined by what we define it as being but rather a Light that defines each of us completely independent of who we think we are. He sees us as who we truly are when oftentimes we can't even see it ourselves.

He sees His creation as in its purest form. He sees our beginning and our seemingly end on this earth which is highlighted by His ability to see past what we can see.

He makes no mistakes.

The world will discourage the boldness our faith. It just will. It will try to cause fear to guide our every step seeking to discourage and contain us. But, as children of His, we were never meant to be contained. We were meant to soar on the wings of eagles, move mountains and stand boldly against the giants of this world. I dare say, however, it will only be when we step outside of our own strength, when we have spent all that we have inside ourselves and we have left everything at His feet that we will experience the greatness of Who He is.

Only then can we soar when the wind and gravity drags us down. Only then can we move mountains that are entrenched in the earth. Only then can we stand firm no matter what we face off against.

Only then can we stand face to face against the mightiest judge in this land and not waver in our faith.

For some of us, it is a life long journey. We lay it down and pick it up. We walk in His strength until we can take it back ourselves. We live in constant upheaval of trying to do it on our own while proclaiming His greatness when; quite honestly, we haven't given Him the latitude to showcase His greatness. We have only experienced the previews.

Today, we stand not only with the choice of Who we follow but we also stand with the necessity of being disciplined enough to follow and allow Him to lead.

Live worthy.

What do you continually try to do in your own strength?

What would it look like if you simply placed it at His feet, not to be picked up again?

What specific action plan can you take today to live worthy?

A Better Life | 1 Timothy 6:17

Command those who are rich in this present world not to be arrogant nor to put their hope in wealth, which is so uncertain, but to put their hope in God, who richly provides us with everything for our enjoyment.

We can be so sure of ourselves. So sure of our life, our schedule, our world and our priorities. We live as if guaranteed tomorrow, guaranteed the rest of today and promised our next breath. We find security in our homes, communities and cars focusing on our achievements and successes or lamenting on what we could or should have had.

Our lives focus on the promises of this world. Promises of happiness and happy ever afters that seem to come true for some and fall short for others. We, to often, guide ourselves by what is seen on TV or mainstream idealizing what it would be like if.

If we had more money.

If we had a better body.

If we had more loving family relationships.

If we better friends, a faster car, more this, more that.

A better life.

If only. If only none of that mattered to us. If only we could look at our life, the cards that we have to play and step up to the plate to play the biggest game of our life.

Because that, dear ones, is what it is. No do overs. One shot.

One shot and then for some of us the opportunity to sit back and reflect on the choices that we've made. Choices that will reflect how the definition on wealth changes as we become closer to our Father. Wealth that the world will tell us must look and smell shiny new but instead is found in a Hope that is older than the world. A Hope that never fades.

Can you imagine a better life than living one that cannot be tarnished, dimmed nor crushed by this world?

A life that is so focused on the Hope of Christ that the rest is just fog that fails to penetrate and simply disappears. That kind of life. A life so steeped in His provisional grace that, looking neither left or right, God's love oozes out of us. Do you feel His love oozing today?

Of course, today is Monday, the kids aren't in school yet, the car broke down, new job, dying parent or child and the list goes on and on. But, these are all things of this world. Each and every one. None eternal. Focus instead on what is eternal and when we only focus there life has a completely different perspective.

A perspective that can't be bought.

Live worthy.

What "cards" have you been dealt in life that you would have liked to have left on the table?

How can you observe each of these through the lens of Eternity? How can they mold you instead of hurt you?

What specific action plan can you take today to live worthy?

Do Good | 1 Timothy 6:18

Command them to do good, to be rich in good deeds and to be generous and willing to share.

Do good and good deeds. Be generous and share.

We do this, yes? However do our lives permeate with this command? Every day. Every moment. It seems to often that we do this as a scheduled event. Next Tuesday, we are going to do a shoe drive. Check. Next Saturday, we are going to take a meal to a family in need. Check. On Sunday, we are scheduled to teach in Sunday School. Check.

Too often, we fulfill this requirement by scheduled obligations. Our calendar is filled with many such obligations. We lived stressed trying to meet them all. Yet, many times the obligation doesn't go much farther than our planner and our hasty drop-off as we quickly move to the next scheduled event to do good because that is what we are supposed to do.

Yet, too often it leaves us drained instead of filling us with joy and we become overwhelmed by what we feel obligated to do instead of experiencing the joy that comes with serving through obedience. It is what is in our heart that God is interested in not what is in the casserole dish.

He has called us to bless someone; to be His hands and feet, for a reason and it isn't because we make the best fried chicken or because we own the fastest lawn mower. He's called us to grow us, to mature our faith and to give us the opportunity to work where

Live Worthy

He is working. A divine appointment.

Something to be treasured not out of duty but out of the pleasure of serving with our Father.

In time, our planner will no longer be filled with scheduled good deeds but rather our lives will become one with goodness. We won't have to schedule it. It will just be.

Live worthy.

What was the last unscheduled good deed that you completed?

How many "scheduled" good deeds are on your calendar for this week?

What specific action plan can you take today to live worthy?

Just One Drop Of Water | 1 Timothy 6:19

In this way they will lay up treasure for themselves as a firm foundation for the coming age, so that they may take hold of the life that is truly life.

So that we might take hold of the life that is truly life.

Hard to imagine, isn't it? A life better than this? A life that is so much more than we live today that it is considered the true life and this is simply the shadows leading up to it.

Hard to imagine.

Especially when we put so much into this life. Creating our world so that it is as perfect as we can make it. We strive to become self-sufficient and self-aware while searching to answer the questions that linger inside our souls. And, yet, this is not our true life.

We create personal masterpieces in the ways of our homes, careers, families, our bodies and sometimes our churches. We expend our time and energy searching for the next big thing, whatever that might be. We are constantly searching for the "thing" that will allow us to arrive, allow us to be still, allow us to fit in and be content.

When God told Noah to build an ark, Noah sat out to obey his command. He built and labored amidst hecklers and unbelievers, yet he stayed steadfast and on point. He knew to Whom he listened.

He knew what really mattered. He knew the voice of His Lord so well that he completed the task without a single drop of rain as encouragement or confirmation. He obeyed.

I'm afraid today many of us would approach the task in a multitude of ways. We would try to walk on both sides of the fence. We would build the ark but we would try to find a way that would also appease the hecklers.

We would find a way suitable to them that would either involve them, entertain them or at the very least be hospitable to them in some manner when sometimes, just maybe, there are to be moments that cause uncomfortableness deep in one's soul. Moments that require a response from the person within instead of being glossed over by others for fear of causing discomfort.

Or, perhaps, we would want to see confirmation. Just one drop of rain. One drop of water. Clouds forming in the distant. We'd get our inner circle together and pray about it and discuss it. We would read books about it. We would gather in the troops with the real builders to oversee it. We would make it our project instead of God's or we wouldn't even make it to the point of making it a project at all.

There is a Voice that speaks directly to our soul. Do we listen? Do we even recognize it and know when to listen? And then how do we react? Our true life awaits. Will we choose to live it?

Live worthy.

What would have been your reaction to building the ark?

How can you adjust your life to live it as God has created you to live?

What specific action plan can you take today to live worthy?

godless chatter. Little g. | 1 Timothy 6: 20-21

Turn away from godless chatter and the opposing ideas of what is falsely called knowledge, which some have professed and in so doing have departed from the faith. Grace be with you all.

How much godless chatter carries on in our lives? How often do we mistake godless chatter for Godly wisdom? How many times do we seek His Words from others and instead hear the chatter of noise.

There is not a shortage of godless chatter in our lives. We don't have to look far. Unfortunately, sometimes it isn't easily recognized. And perhaps, those are the most dangerous words, the chatter that masquerades as Truth. Many times, it is found in those closest to us. Those who speak more out of love of emotions from their hearts than the Truth that feeds our soul.

They mean well.

Maybe you two weren't really meant to be together.

God just wants you to be happy.

She's now an angel.

You deserve a break today.

And the list goes on and on. And while it may soothe our heart, it misleads our soul and those around us. Truth. That is what we must seek. Truth and Truth alone. Even when it hurts. Even when it means seeking the path least traveled that appears heavily burdened with thorns.

Truth will set us free instead of placing us in the bondage of carefully disguised words that offer fleeting comfort and direction.

We must seek those who we know are daily in their Bibles. Those who seek Him above all else for guidance. Those who will guide not from their hearts or their own pride but rather from His direction. His Words. Not watered down. Not afraid yet real.

In times past, it was a matter of a person's life or death to know just how real ones Christian friends were. To confide in one who masqueraded as a Christian, yet was really just setting a trap could result in the loss of ones life. Today, most of us don't have the fear that speaking about our faith will result in the loss of our lives, however possibly we live falsely secure. We don't seem to have to evaluate those in whom we confide in as closely. Do their lives exhibit the Fruits of the Spirit? Do they walk the talk?

Many have been deceived by those who wear proudly the label of Christian yet have very little, if any, outwardly overflow of His grace and mercy in their lives. We must be wise and purposeful seeking Truth always. It's not being politically correct. It is choosing to be real. A title or a following doesn't mean Truth. The presence of Jesus does.

Seek wisely.

Live worthy.

Are you easily corrected?

How do you know that those you confide in are steeped in Truth?

What specific action plan can you take today to live worthy?

Today is the last day.

'Living Worthy' is so much more than just pages on a book. It was the journey that came out of the valley of our daughter's death. It was the reality of coming face-to-face with our Heavenly Father and realizing the magnitude of Who He really is. Within the blink of an eye, He called her home. Within one breath, He had the power to pull her from this earth and into the heavenly realm. This took my breath away. This made Him ever so much more real, majestic and Holy.

And, yet, what was I?

Her death made me realize even more so that some day, I too would stand before the King. I wanted to live such a life that not only would I hear "Well done, good and faithful servant." but that also my life would be one that would live worthy of being called one of His. This changed my entire mindset. No longer concerned with earthly standards that extended so much pseudo-grace but rather concerned with His standards that needed to provide the framework of my life.

Yes, her death changed me but His Words have changed me even more. I pray that you have found the same desire and challenge to live worthy not because it's required but because He is Who He is. Each and every day. This book followed our journey to a full year without her on this earth. He walked with us every step of the way.

Which leads us to the next book, 'Live Different" taken from 2 Timothy. What does it look like to truly live worthy? How do we set aside what the world tells and look full-face into Him?

So thank each of you for your encouragement, prayers and unwavering support as we continue on this journey. The proceeds from the book will be used to help support our ministry in the field and Project H.O.P.E. What an amazing answer to prayer! I ask for each of your prayers in this endeavor. We serve an amazing God.

Therefore, tomorrow, we straighten our shoulders and we carry on.

We will choose to live worthy of the call He has put upon our lives. Steeped in mercy and grace, shoulder's squared in sheer obedience, we carry on.

Project H.O.P.E.

Project H.O.P.E. is an inter-denominational service organization dedicated to meeting the immediate physical needs of impoverished people, while sharing with them the Good News of Jesus Christ. Serving the poorest of the poor in Nicaragua and Haiti, Project H.O.P.E. strives to serve so that everyone might know Him.

In 1998, Project H.O.P.E. was established after a group of friends felt God calling them to help the poor in Nicaragua. The founding directors had been traveling to Nicaragua for a few years, but felt called to do more than build homes and return to the United States. There was a need to share the Gospel with the people of Nicaragua.

Project H.O.P.E.'s very humble beginning consisted of the directors and their wives traveling to Nicaragua and slowly others joined. Some trips consisted of camping in the mountains and bathing in the river. God has blessed Project H.O.P.E. greatly. Over 700 people travel with Project H.O.P.E. each year. A full-functioning base camp, H.O.P.E. Central Nicaragua was built in 2006. In 2013, we began construction at H.O.P.E. Central Haiti. Both facilities serve as a headquarters for our in-country staff and housing for short-term mission teams.

For those that are interested in a personal boots-on-the-ground mission experience, contact Project H.O.P.E. at pjhope.org and come serve with us bringing Matthew 25:35-36 to life.

project HOPE
pjhope.org

For I was hungry and you gave me something to eat, I was thirsty and you gave me something to drink, I was a stranger and you invited me in, I needed clothes and you clothed me, I was sick and you looked after me, I was in prison and you came to visit me.

Serving as an outreach to single mothers and their children, Taellor's House provides after school care for children along with various programs for mothers. Many school-age children are unable to attend school because they are taking care of their younger siblings while their mother is at work. Taellor's House provides care for preschool children as well, allowing the older children to attend school. Children receive lunch (Monday-Friday), tutoring, biblical teaching, English classes, a school uniform, and school supplies. Mothers receive biblical parenting skills, vocational skills, and help securing a job. Taellor's House began operation in 2016 and now serves over 100 children and 58 families.

Internship opportunities are also be available for girls over the age of 18 who are interested in long-term mission work.

Taellor's House is named after Taellor Stearns, who passed away in June 2014 at the age of 19. She was a missionary to Nicaragua and part of the Project H.O.P.E. family. Taellor had a passion for children and was excited about the children's center project. It was only fitting that the center was named after her.

For those interested in hearing more about Taellor's House or intern positions, contact Project H.O.P.E. at pjhope.org.

I remember so vividly the night that Taellor died. So vividly. I remember coming home, telling Slaton, greeting the friends who had come to walk the journey with us, going to my room and as the boys lay sleeping, I remember thinking, "How?"

"How will I ever leave them alone again? How will I ever serve You to my wild abandonment? How will I ever laugh again? How will I ever feel joy again? How will I ever face a world that is so tainted in death? How will I trust again? How will I ever just be again? How can I breath normally? How will I ever answer my phone again? How can I see past the tears and hurt? How can I be who You have created me to be through this?"

And I remember thinking, quite selfishly...., "I will so miss this name, Father. A name You gave us, as unique as she was created, it will be forever gone."

And as satan, true to form, kept whispering doubts, God kept directing me to Psalm 139. He knew. He knew the number of her days. He knew them before she was ever born.

This journey that we walk is a journey that, as those who are walking it also, is not easy. It is an every day, sometimes, every moment, every breath battle. It will be until the day I meet my Savior face to face. It will just be. A battle not between flesh and blood but in the spiritual realm.

A battle in which God has remained ever faithful.

He has shown us how to find joy again. How to laugh, even amongst tears perhaps, but how to laugh, how to serve with wild abandonment, how to set it all aside, even amidst the fear and worry, and say, "This is all Yours...and not just say it but to take action upon it." As I've responded before, even as you observe our walk of obedience, make no mistake, I miss her more than there are stars in the sky or sands upon the earth.

The smile, the laughter, the wittiness, the servant, the daughter, the friend...yet, God has given us continual peace that none of that has been lost to us but is now being experienced fully in all the splendors of heaven.

And as icing on the cake, just because He can, He has taken that name that He bestowed on her so uniquely and is using it daily to bring Hope. When I see it, when I type it, I don't feel pride nor entitlement, but rather I feel the magnitude of His grace and mercy as He does what only He can do. The name no longer simply represents a young girl that solely wanted to serve her King by loving on the children He placed before her but rather represents His Hand, His Mighty Hand upon this earth.

Live Worthy

Absolutely breathtaking.

Our journey through the valley of grief is written in *Know Hope* also available on Amazon.

Thank you for walking this journey with us. We chose to publish this book independently in order to maintain the original writings just as they were written when we were daily walking the journey through the first year after. Words written raw everyday. Words written through tears and unspeakable pain. Yet, words that brought comfort and joy as God continued to be faithful. The devotions continue through the second year after her death in Live Different due out towards the end of 2019.

You can continue to follow our journey at Tammy Conner Stearns on Facebook or contact us at stearnstammy@ymail.com to share your own journey.

I am also available for speaking engagements.

May we find Hope through Him always.

Live Worthy

Made in the USA
Columbia, SC
15 June 2019